*G*ranite boulders shelter coconut palms on La Digue, one of the isles of the Seychelles in the Indian Ocean.

FOLLOWING PAGES: *An Indonesian sunset lights the way home for Balinese fishermen paddling a jukung.*

MAJESTIC
ISLAND
WORLDS

Prepared by the Special Publications Division
National Geographic Society, Washington, D.C.

MAJESTIC ISLAND WORLDS

Contributing Authors: LESLIE ALLEN, RON FISHER,
CHRISTINE ECKSTROM LEE, TOM MELHAM,
THOMAS O'NEILL, CYNTHIA RUSS RAMSAY
Contributing Photographers: SAM ABELL, PAUL VON BAICH,
PAUL CHESLEY, BILL CURTSINGER, NICHOLAS DEVORE III,
SCOTT RUTHERFORD, MICHAEL S. YAMASHITA

Published by THE NATIONAL GEOGRAPHIC SOCIETY
GILBERT M. GROSVENOR, *President and Chairman of the Board*
MELVIN M. PAYNE, THOMAS W. MCKNEW, *Chairmen Emeritus*
OWEN R. ANDERSON, *Executive Vice President*
ROBERT L. BREEDEN, *Senior Vice President, Publications
and Educational Media*

Prepared by THE SPECIAL PUBLICATIONS DIVISION
DONALD J. CRUMP, *Director*
PHILIP B. SILCOTT, *Associate Director*
BONNIE S. LAWRENCE, *Assistant Director*
MARY ANN HARRELL, *Contributing Editor*

Staff for this Book
RICHARD M. CRUM, *Managing Editor*
CHARLES E. HERRON, *Illustrations Editor*
JODY BOLT, *Art Director*
ALICE JABLONSKY, *Senior Researcher and Project Coordinator*
ELIZABETH W. FISHER, MARIA MUDD,
ELIZABETH P. SCHLEICHERT, JAYNE WISE, *Researchers*
RON FISHER, ALICE JABLONSKY, CHRISTINE ECKSTROM LEE,
JANE R. MCCAULEY, THOMAS O'NEILL,
CYNTHIA RUSS RAMSAY, JENNIFER C. URQUHART,
Picture Legend Writers
TIBOR TOTH, *Map Artist*
JOSEPH F. OCHLAK, *Map Editor*
ROSAMUND GARNER, *Editorial Assistant*
ARTEMIS S. LAMPATHAKIS, *Illustrations Assistant*

Engraving, Printing, and Product Manufacture
ROBERT W. MESSER, *Manager*
GEORGE V. WHITE, *Assistant Manager*
DAVID V. SHOWERS, *Production Manager*
GEORGE J. ZELLER, JR., *Production Project Manager*
GREGORY STORER, *Senior Assistant Production Manager*
LEWIS R. BASSFORD, MARK R. DUNLEVY,
Assistant Production Managers
TIMOTHY H. EWING, *Production Assistant*
CAROL R. CURTIS, *Senior Production Staff Assistant*
MARY ELIZABETH ELLISON, LESLIE CAROL,
SANDRA F. LOTTERMAN, ELIZA C. MORTON,
VALERIE A. WOODS, *Staff Assistants*

MAUREEN WALSH, *Indexer*

Library of Congress CIP Data: page 199.

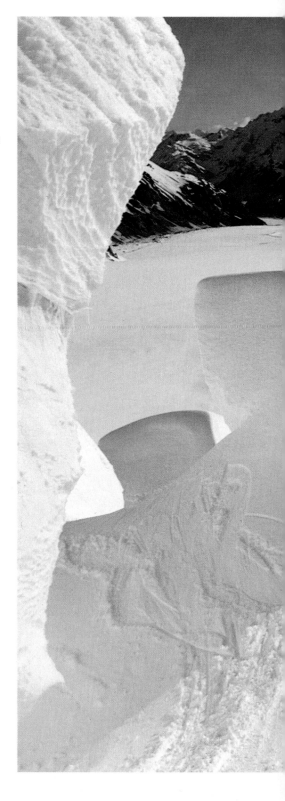

*Snowbound splendor of New Zealand's
Tasman Glacier envelops a skier in the
Southern Alps. Lovers of the outdoors
thrill to this island nation's high peaks
and fast-running rivers.*

4

Trawlers ride the morning calm of low tide in Dingle Harbour on Ireland's westernmost peninsula. The boats carry crews fishing for herring and species of whitefish off the island's rugged coast.

INTRODUCTION
Lands Surrounded by the Sea

By Ron Fisher

Eroding and subsiding, Moorea will eventually slip beneath the waters of the South Pacific. It will leave behind its azure lagoon ringed by wave-washed coral, an island known as an atoll.

Come island-hopping with me. . . . On Tenerife, in the Canary Islands, I'm standing at a roadside and gazing at a shoreline far below, where Atlantic surf breaks on lava boulders. In an apricot tree immediately before me, three small gray birds with yellowish breasts alight and start singing. They are—what else?—canaries.

But don't be misled. The islands were named not for the birds but for large native dogs once found here: *Canis* became Canaria became Canary, and the birds inherited the name. Oddities like this are part of the fun of islands, part of the individuality that can make even a small island a world in its own right.

Over the years, I've been lucky enough to visit quite a few islands. I've explored the Hawaiian group. I've exchanged moody stares with the stone statues of Easter Island, remnants of the sort of puzzling island culture that can develop when generations pass without contact from overseas. I've been dripped on in the rain forests of the Queen Charlotte Islands off the west coast of Canada, where aged, moss-covered totems still brood. I've trod the crusty lava flows of Iceland, where even the sunsets seem cold and distant, and I've dozed against coconut palms in Tahiti, where the sun seems to set in your lap and the clouds threaten to burst into flame. I've sweltered in the scurry and bustle of Hong Kong, island of commerce. And I've heard the clang of a cell door slamming shut on the prison island of Alcatraz: Isolation is no guarantee of paradise.

An island, geographers say, is any area of land surrounded by water. Then what about Australia? No. It's so big it's considered an island continent. Greenland at 840,000 square miles ranks as the world's largest island, while islets shade off into rocks at the other end of the scale.

Some experts sort the world's uncountable islands into two broad categories: oceanic and continental. Oceanic islands are usually born of volcanic eruption, far from major landmasses. Such is Bouvet, uninhabited and alone in the South Atlantic: perhaps the most isolated of all, with no land for a thousand miles in any direction. Continental islands have become separated from—naturally—continents, and therefore can boast of an ancient and varied geologic history. Their island identity, however, may begin with the recent Ice Age: As the ice sheets melted, the sea level rose and flooded low-lying coasts, marooning such high ground as the British Isles, Sri Lanka, Newfoundland, and Manhattan.

In fact, islands originate in many ways. Often their formation stems from the workings of plate tectonics: the ponderous movement of tremendous plates of rock in the earth's crust, floating upon a denser, hotter subterranean layer. It's their pulling apart and pushing together that reshape landmasses. Forces generated by this titanic movement break off majestic islands like Madagascar from continental rims and uplift others, like Japan, along the edges of the plates.

When an oceanic plate moves over a "hot spot" in the underlying layer, molten rock may build up one volcanic island after another in a linear chain—the Hawaiian group and the Galápagos are good examples. Other volcanic islands, such as Iceland, form along great rifts in the ocean floor where plates are pulling apart and releasing molten rock from far below.

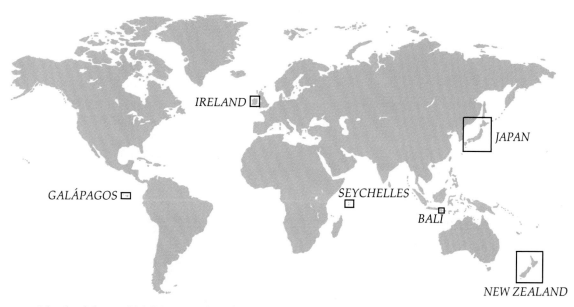

Islands of the world fall into two broad classes, say scientists. Continental isles, such as Ireland, are those that have been separated from a continent. Oceanic islands, such as the Galápagos, are those usually born of fire far from land.

And in the tropics, a volcanic island may erode while colonies of coral build upon its debris in the shallows; they grow toward the sunlight, forming a fringing reef. Eventually the cone wears away, leaving the coral around a central lagoon. Often these coral atolls are the loveliest of islands, jewel-like specks of sun-bright surf in a dark immensity of sea.

Biologically, islands are populated by a process called distribution. Even Bouvet has penguins and seals. Elsewhere, plants and land animals arrive on winds and tides or on rafts of vegetation swept out to sea by floods and storms. In time, descendants of these survivors may lose their potential for dispersal. Thus a species of cormorant in the Galápagos, without natural predators there, has lost the need and therefore the ability to fly.

People, too, are molded by islands—by "happy isles" of natural abundance as well as by storm-pummeled outposts in the high latitudes. Archaeologist Jacquetta Hawkes has written: "An island always has a potent effect on its inhabitants. Its frontiers are immutable, divinely determined rather than due to mere human vicissitudes. Strangers cannot easily cross them unnoticed or unopposed. This sense of being sea-protected, 'the envy of less happier lands,' gives island people a sharp awareness of their identity and of their difference from everyone else. . . . An island home . . . greatly enhances that belief in belonging to a chosen race. . . ."

For this book, we selected a diverse handful: Japan, a combination of subtle Oriental beauty and energetic trade; Ireland, realm of misty days and haunting charm; Bali, a place where life is a ceremony from cradle to cremation; New Zealand, an outdoorsman's dreamland; the Seychelles, a tropical paradise flavored by African, Asian, and European cultures.

But to begin, we go to a group of islands where the mysterious origin of species challenged the imagination and changed human thought and history. It's a Pacific archipelago on the Equator, a place, according to Herman Melville, where "no voice, no low, no howl is heard; the chief sound of life here is a hiss." The Galápagos.

11

*H*idden fires of creation send steam
and smoke billowing from New
Zealand's White Island, in the Bay of
Plenty. The island erupts almost

constantly, a showcase of an earth-building process. Fountains of heat help create oceanic islands as lava, flowing from vents in the ocean floor, cools and gradually builds toward the surface. Some lava isles vanish in cataclysmic eruption; others endure, their slopes home to bountiful varieties of life.

14

$\mathcal{E}$nd-of-the-world islands feature 100-foot-tall palms, tool-using finches, seagoing lizards, and many other living oddities found nowhere else on the planet. Opposite: Flightless cormorants and a marine iguana share the sunset on one of the Galápagos Islands (above). The researches of naturalist Charles Darwin brought fame to this volcanic archipelago in the Pacific.

FOLLOWING PAGES: On the island of Madagascar, off the southeast coast of Africa, a grove of baobabs bristles in the fading light of day. A continental isle, Madagascar has drifted eastward, carrying with it six species of baobab; the mainland counts only one. The trunks of these barrel trees can store thousands of gallons of water, occasionally tapped in the dry season by islanders.

15

GALÁPAGOS
Stark Worlds of Wildlife

By Ron Fisher. Photographs by Sam Abell.

*Sea mist wreathes Isla Cowley, one of
scores of isles in the Galápagos
archipelago. Home to bizarre wildlife,
the remote island chain straddles the
Equator 600 miles west of Ecuador.*

Fritz Angermeyer built his first boat when he was eight years old. His brother Karl, two years older, helped. The boat tipped over, so they added sand ballast. Too much ballast. The boat sank. That was many years ago. Later, when they were young men, Fritz, Karl, and their three brothers bought a more seaworthy boat and sailed away from Hamburg, Germany, to see the world. They arrived in the Galápagos Islands in 1937 and made lives for themselves by farming, fishing, and, when tourists began arriving, by chartering boats.

It had long been a dream of mine to visit the Galápagos, those enchanted isles at world's end, and my chance came one recent summer. Renowned for their singular wildlife and their austere beauty, the Galápagos are as remote as they are bizarre. Bearing a mix of old English and Spanish names, they lie on the Equator about 600 miles off the coast of Ecuador, a group of 13 major and 6 minor islands and scores of small, nameless rocks. All are volcanic, born of a geologic hot spot on the ocean floor during the last five million years. They total approximately 3,000 square miles of land in 23,000 square miles of ocean, a land area less than the size of Connecticut broken in pieces and scattered across a body of water nearly the length and breadth of West Virginia.

The impression persists that the Galápagos are uninhabited, so I was unprepared to find about 10,000 people, mostly Ecuadorians, living permanently on four of the islands. The largest settlement, numbering about 4,000 people, is Puerto Ayora on Isla Santa Cruz, where the three remaining Angermeyer brothers live. Now in their 70s, they have homes built of lava overlooking Academy Bay, and Fritz is still building boats. A 45-foot vessel of his own design rests on supports in his yard. When I saw it, the hull was complete and the deck was coming along nicely. It looked sleek and powerful and was very beautiful. How long have you been working on it, I asked Fritz. He thought a minute, then smiled and said, "Since I was eight."

It is being built mostly of *matazarno*, a heavy, iron-hard wood from a tree that grows in the arid zone of Santa Cruz. Even the hundreds of six-inch wooden screws that hold the boat together are hand-turned by Fritz on machines he designed and built. In his home, a plaque with a quotation from John Steinbeck reads: "A man builds the best of himself into a boat—builds many of the unconscious memories of his ancestors."

Next door, Karl can often be seen on his veranda, beneath an arbor where warblers chirp, keeping an eye on the comings and goings in the harbor. About a hundred marine iguanas, seagoing lizards some three feet long, live on and around his house. When he has visitors, he feeds the animals—cooked rice, the day I was there. *"Kommen sie, kommen sie,"* he calls, banging pots. A mad scramble ensues, as iguanas come scurrying. They pile atop one another, scratching and biting in their fury to get at the food. They climb headfirst down the walls from the roof where they have been lying spread-eagled in the sun. One has rice smeared on its nose; it can smell it but can't find it. Others lick rice greedily off one another's faces.

Karl has been a Galápagos character for more than half a century. He has guided underwater explorer Jacques Cousteau around the islands, and also Britain's Prince Philip. "When the prince visited in 1970," said Karl, "he wanted to see a land iguana. I knew there was one living in my sister-in-law Carmen's chicken yard, so I took him over there. 'Do you know where you are?' I asked. 'I know, I know,' he said. 'I've already stepped in some.' "

As you ascend the slope of Santa Cruz's central ridge, the vegetation changes. Leaving the arid coast, you climb through increasingly lush countryside, where moisture-laden clouds from the southeast bump into the mountain. An agricultural zone has been set aside there, where farmers grow fruit and vegetables, and a hundred or so ranchers herd about 14,000 head of cattle. Ecuadorian law forbids importing cattle into the islands—there's a danger of introducing pests or diseases—so government agencies allow cattlemen to improve their stock through artificial insemination.

Farther up the slopes, the vegetation changes again. Ferns and orchids grow thick beneath trees hung with mosses and epiphytes. An evergreen shrub, *Miconia*, clothes the hillsides with a nearly impenetrable blanket. Photographer Sam Abell and I walked upward through it one rainy day with Felipe Cruz, slipping and sliding along a dirt road slick with mud, as a steady drizzle fell. A native of the islands, Felipe had developed an interest in birds while collecting finch specimens for a visiting ornithologist. Now he is employed by the Charles Darwin Research Station, inaugurated in 1964 to promote conservation, conduct research, and disseminate information related to the Galápagos. Four years later the Ecuadorian Galápagos National Park Service was created. Almost all the islands' land area is included within the boundaries of the park.

Tall, dark, and bearded, Felipe led us through the dripping trees to a cabin, where his wife, Justine, served us coffee. For several years, Felipe and Justine have been studying the nocturnal dark-rumped, or Hawaiian, petrel. "It's the only officially endangered bird in the islands," Felipe said. "There was a time when you couldn't sleep here in the highlands for the sound of them. During the day they nest in deep earthy burrows, where pigs and rats can get at them, so their numbers have decreased tragically."

Felipe and Justine monitor about 50 burrows, spending weeks at a time in the highlands' drizzle and mist. Sloshing through a mini-torrent in a narrow gully, we followed them. Felipe stopped at the mouth of a burrow, reached into the soft bank up to his shoulder, and pulled out a bird. By the beak! Where the beak goes, I guess, the bird is sure to follow, but it seemed a good way to get pecked. The Cruzes put the bird—about the size of a pigeon—into a small canvas bag and weighed it, then measured a wing, a leg, the beak, and the tail. When they returned the petrel to the burrow, you could hear it muttering to itself as it disappeared.

Günther Reck, a robust German, has been 12 years in the Galápagos, two and a half of them as director of the Darwin Research Station. A big part of his job involves dealing with exotic plants and animals—species that have been either deliberately or accidentally introduced over the years. "The good news is," he told me, "the numbers aren't increasing as fast as they once were. We're holding our own and even making some progress with goats and pigs. They've been eliminated from several of the islands." Captain David Porter, in his account of a visit to the Galápagos in the early 1800s, wrote of putting three females and one male ashore on Santiago.

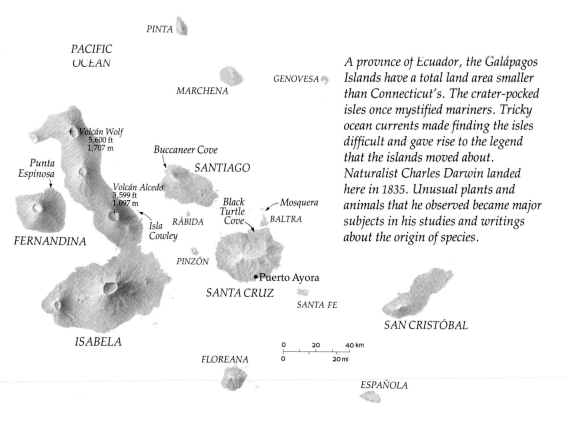

PINTA

PACIFIC
OCEAN

MARCHENA

GENOVESA

Volcán Wolf
5,600 ft
1,707 m

Buccaneer Cove

Punta
Espinosa

SANTIAGO

Volcán Alcedo
3,599 ft
1,097 m

Black
Turtle
Cove

Mosquera

BALTRA

Isla
Cowley

RÁBIDA

FERNANDINA

PINZÓN

•Puerto Ayora

SANTA CRUZ

SANTA FE

SAN CRISTÓBAL

ISABELA

FLOREANA

0   20   40 km
0   20 mi

ESPAÑOLA

A province of Ecuador, the Galápagos Islands have a total land area smaller than Connecticut's. The crater-pocked isles once mystified mariners. Tricky ocean currents made finding the isles difficult and gave rise to the legend that the islands moved about. Naturalist Charles Darwin landed here in 1835. Unusual plants and animals that he observed became major subjects in his studies and writings about the origin of species.

"Future navigators may perhaps obtain here an abundant supply of goats' meat; for unmolested as they will be . . . it is probable their increase will be very rapid." Today there are an estimated 100,000 feral goats on Santiago.

The station, in conjunction with the Galápagos National Park Service, assesses the effect of tourism on the Galápagos. Ecuadorian officials today suggest that the number of tourists visiting the islands be limited to 25,000 a year, and some officials worry that that's too many. "The danger," said Günther, "is that the Ecuadorian government might begin to think that tourism in the Galápagos can save the country's economy. It can't do that, but with improved management support we could handle a few more tourists here. It's possible to look at animals without harming them."

Scientists from all over the world come to study the ecology of the islands, and undergraduates come to assist. I met one of them, Ecuadorian biology student Ana Sancho, among the tortoises at the station. Weighing as much as 600 pounds, the Galápagos tortoises—together with those on Aldabra in the Seychelles—are the world's largest living tortoises. There were once 14 distinct subspecies in the archipelago, but now there are 11, all threatened by loss of habitat and predation by exotic animals. Each race had its own island or habitat where it evolved independently. This shows up most clearly in their carapaces: The shape depends, at least in part, on the food source. On the isles where food grows some distance off the ground, the tortoise shell is shaped in such a way that the tortoise can crane its neck and reach up high; in contrast, on lusher islands, the shell design features a tighter fitting collar, since a tortoise need only stick its neck straight out and move it from side to side to eat the food growing a few inches high. Probably all Galápagos tortoises evolved from a common stock, animals that reached the islands hundreds of thousands of years ago, perhaps on rafts of floating vegetation from mainland rivers.

In an effort to help the threatened tortoises, the research station assists the park service in breeding captive animals, hatching the eggs, rearing the young for several years, then freeing them on their respective islands. About 900 young tortoises have been released. I found Ana surrounded by pens full of baby tortoises. They ranged in size from silver dollars to small dinner plates. Of the smallest, 99 were fast asleep, but the 100th was trucking across the bodies of its sleeping peers, on some vital errand.

Scientists are unable to determine the sex of a newborn tortoise without killing it, Ana told me. They believe the temperature of the nest may be the factor that decides the sex, so some of the station's eggs are put in incubators kept near 79°F—a temperature that should produce females. Other eggs are stored at about 92°F—and should be hot-blooded males. "After all," said Ana, as she carefully buried a fresh batch of Española Island eggs in plastic dishpans full of cushioning vermiculite, "if we raise tortoises that are all the same sex, it doesn't go far toward solving the problem of their dwindling numbers." The incubators were plywood chests, like clothes closets, with hair dryers inside rigged to thermostats. In the wild, biologists believe, the depth of the nest and the position of the eggs within it provide the critical temperatures for determining sex.

The first scientist to study the tortoises was Charles Darwin, the Galápagos' most famous visitor. He arrived in 1835 as naturalist aboard H.M.S. *Beagle*. Neither Darwin nor the captain, Robert FitzRoy, was much impressed with his first view of the islands. "A shore fit for pandemonium," wrote FitzRoy. And Darwin noted: "Nothing could be less inviting than the first appearance. A broken field of black basaltic lava . . . crossed by great fissures, is everywhere covered by stunted sunburnt brushwood."

The *Beagle* spent five weeks in the Galápagos, busy weeks for Darwin. He was able to go ashore on only five of the islands, but from those five he collected specimens—and lingering impressions. A local official told him he could tell which island a giant tortoise came from just by looking at it. Also, Darwin noticed, many of the plants and animals were similar to those of the South American mainland, yet different. What's more, they differed slightly from island to island. Certain finches, for instance, seemed to have beaks especially suited to the food available in their particular habitat. A finch with a long, slightly curved bill probed fleshy cactus pulp; one with a thick, powerful bill cracked open hard seeds and fed on them; another, with a bill like a sparrow's, plucked ticks and mites from reptiles.

"Seeing this gradation and diversity of structure in one small, intimately related group of birds," Darwin would later write, "one might really fancy that from an original paucity of birds in this archipelago, one species had been taken and modified for different ends." Darwin was groping toward the concept now called adaptive radiation: that animals, isolated long enough, will evolve to fit their particular habitat. He went home to England, and for nearly 25 years he pondered the wildlife that he had seen on

23

his travels before publishing the great work that laid the foundations for modern biology: *On the Origin of Species*. His theories show up even today in our newspapers and courts, and the whole process began for Darwin on a distant shoreline. In the Galápagos he wrote, "both in space and time, we seem to be brought somewhat near to that great fact—that mystery of mysteries—the first appearance of new beings on this earth."

By the time of Darwin's visit in 1835, the islands were well known to the world's mariners. In 1535, a Dominican friar named Tomás de Berlanga, on a mission to Peru for the king of Spain, drifted into the Galápagos group. He later wrote of "many seals, turtles, iguanas, tortoises, many birds like those of Spain, but so silly that they do not know how to flee. . . ."

Tricky currents often made finding the Galápagos difficult, and the legend arose that they floated randomly around the Pacific. In the 16th century, Spanish explorers referred to the Galápagos as *Las Islas Encantadas*: The Enchanted Isles. (Novelist Herman Melville picked up the name in 1856 for his account of the islands.) Buccaneers and pirates used the Galápagos as a refuge during the 17th and 18th centuries, and whaling ships arrived in great numbers in the first half of the 19th century. More than 30 called at Floreana alone in 1834. For the seafarers, the islands provided an easy source of fresh meat—the giant tortoises that lumbered across the lava fields. Hauled aboard ship and stored in the hold, or even on their backs on deck, they lived for months without food or water and could be slaughtered as needed. Perhaps a hundred thousand were taken. By the early 20th century they were extinct on Floreana and Santa Fe.

Few but scientists visited the Galápagos for the next fifty years, but the outbreak of World War II gave the islands a sudden strategic importance. The Panama Canal, just a thousand miles to the northeast, was vital to Allied shipping, and fears arose that Japan might use the islands as a base from which to attack it. In the summer of 1942, the United States began constructing an air base on Baltra. When it closed in 1947, the Ecuadorian air force occupied the site, and today most visitors to the islands touch down on the resurfaced main runway.

The town of Puerto Ayora is in the midst of a boom, with new buildings going up, new boats being built, new shops opening. Tourists explore the gravelly streets, shopping for T-shirts and black coral jewelry. The venturesome visit the smoky pool hall or the disco, where American rock thumps and whines half the night. Because of the international nature of the visitors, many Puerto Ayorans know a few words of several languages, which can give their conversation a colorful twist. One evening, when we happened to witness a shooting star, traditionally the time for the making of wishes, my Ecuadorian guide said: "Did you ask a desire?"

Early one morning I helped Sam haul his camera gear down to a Puerto Ayora dock. Offshore bobbed the boats that visitors charter to the other islands. The one Sam and I took was *Cachalote,* Spanish for sperm whale. A converted salmon fishing boat from California, it was skippered by Federico "Fiddi" Angermeyer, Fritz's son. With him on board was Mike Durban, a naturalist-guide in the Galápagos. In the weeks ahead, barefooted Mike would lead us up and down volcanoes and across jagged lava.

We had arrived in the islands in summer, the season that the Ecua-dorians call *garua*, or mist. A time of cooler days and rougher oceans, garua means wet clouds hovering day after day in the highlands. As we toured the islands, we often found ourselves in pale, moist clouds. They were seldom thick enough to get us very wet, and they helped keep the sunburn to a minimum and the temperature in the comfort zone. But away from the mis-ty islands, in the open sea, the equatorial sun beat down and the sea spar-kled. Out of the deep blue depths dolphins came, like sleek gray torpedoes. You could hear them whistle and click as they played at *Cachalote*'s plunging bow. They seemed to swim with no effort at all, racing ahead of the boat, then falling back and taking position again at the bow. They rolled over onto their sides and peered up at us, then leaped clear of the water and fell back with a splash. One day a group was there, then suddenly gone. They reap-peared a mile or so away, where a school of fish set off a feeding frenzy. Overhead, a hundred boobies and frigatebirds circled and dove. Fat peli-cans skimmed across the waves or bobbed in the swell, and the dolphins ca-vorted among them. It reminded me of films of naval battles, with both the sky and the sea full of activity.

Nearly everywhere we went, we were welcomed by sea lions. Go-ing ashore in the neoprene dinghy, we would find them at our elbows. Be-whiskered, brown-eyed, sleek, and black, they were curious and friendly. They swam on their backs under the dinghy and gazed up at us. At night, they played around the anchored *Cachalote*, trailing clouds of phosphores-cence as they swam up to the portholes. I could hear them out there in the starry darkness, snorting and splashing. One day we anchored the dinghy at the beach of Mosquera, a thin sand bar, and waded ashore. When we re-turned, frolicking sea lions had moved the anchor chain several yards from shore, and Mike had to swim through a cluster of them to retrieve it.

Ashore, the females and young lead lives of peaceful ease, dozing in the warm sun. Their whiskers twitch as they dream, and, awak-ened, they watch you with flirtatious eyes. Or they look back at you over their slim shoulders, shyly. Or they sit on their haunches, bend their heads over backward, and look at you upside down. Coming ashore, they lurch up the sand and across lava boulders for a few yards, then collapse in a heap. Offshore, truculent bulls patrol their territories, swimming back and forth, endlessly bellowing as they guard their harems.

At Punta Espinosa on Fernandina, a pup only a few hours old got its first swimming lesson. Barely bigger than a loaf of bread, it cried as its moth-er tried to lure it into the water. It wiggled and squirmed and bleated like a lamb, then gathered its courage and plunged in. Its huge mother nudged it back and forth in the water for a bit, then picked it up by the back of the neck and set it ashore.

Their lives look perfect, but aren't: On Floreana, one lay dying on the beach, a bloody gash in its side, flies in its eyes. Sharks, too, haunt the Galápagos waters. We saw a school of 30 of the white-tipped variety resting immobile on the bottom of a mangrove-rimmed lagoon on Santa Cruz. They were four or five feet long. The tide was out and the water just a couple of feet deep. A pelican landed with a splash among them, saw where it was, and—whoa!—backpedaled furiously. When the shadow of the dinghy passed across them, they gave a flick of their tails and were instantly gone.

In Black Turtle Cove, also on Santa Cruz, a score of golden rays drifted through the clear water in perfect unison, stacked and spaced like a squadron of bombers. Sea turtles, dark circles that flew like birds through the water, poked their black, knobby heads up for a breath of air. Until recently, they faced a new threat in the islands. The building boom in Puerto Ayora prompted builders to bag sand from remote beaches to use with their cement. At one inland construction site, doomed sea turtle hatchlings emerged from the pile of sand. Extraction of beach sand is now prohibited.

Going ashore on most of the islands, we entered a largely drab world: black lava, gray sand, ghostly *palo santo* trees, cactus a washed-out green or brown. Sally Lightfoot crabs, named for their tiptoe scuttle across short stretches of water, provide a splash of color. Bright red and orange, they wash in waves across the lava as surf breaks across them.

Their partners in the surf are the Galápagos's oddest inhabitants, the marine iguanas. The world's only seagoing lizards, they are black, ugly, lethargic. Captain the Right Honourable Lord Byron, the poet's cousin, called them "imps of darkness" in 1825. They have the sort of faces that come slithering toward you in nightmares. But despite their fierce looks, they are tame and harmless. Iguanas nibble on algae growing on the rocks at water's edge or swim out and dive to feed on the bottom. Ashore, they lie sprawled across one another, soaking up sun to heat their cold blood. Occasionally, they sneeze a cloud of vapor out of their nostrils, expelling salt. Their tracks in the sand—footprints straddling a groove made by their dragging tails—look like zippers. Naturalist William Beebe, who visited the islands in the 1920s, wrote of one: "As far as appearances went, he might have been as old as the lava."

They swim by wagging their heavy tails. From the cliffs at Punta Vincente Roca, we looked far down to the sea; the surf, with iguanas mixed in, came crashing ashore. The water was pale blue, full of lather, and the animals seemed helpless and tiny in its swirl. But when the foam from a breaking wave cleared, there they were, clinging to a boulder, dripping.

For years the Galápagos have attracted birdwatchers—for there are plenty of birds to watch. Of the 58 resident species, 28 are endemic, appearing nowhere else. Another 76 species have been recorded. At sea, frigatebirds soar high in the sky and when the opportunity arises, swoop down to snatch morsels from the water with surgical precision. Their wing area is greater, relative to their body weight, than that of any other bird: About a quarter of a pound of skeleton supports a wing span of eight feet, so they're mostly feathers—and fury. They attack other seabirds, especially boobies, in midair, forcing them to disgorge their food. I saw a booby and a frigate both clinging to the same piece of fish. When the frigate tried to fly off with it, the booby went limp and simply dangled. Three kinds of boobies live in the Galápagos: masked, red-footed, and blue-footed—my favorites. All feed at sea. They fly along, then fold themselves into a trident shape and drop headfirst into the sea. All are about the size of ducks. Masked boobies are the prettiest, mostly white; the red-footed nest in trees, their webbed feet awkwardly wrapped around branches; and the blue-footed nest on the ground, in a circle of dung and a few twigs.

Günther Reck had told me, "Boobies were born to be looked at." Stroll through a colony of nesting blue-foots and you provoke some whistles and honks, but they stand their ground, scowling and looking you up and down as if deciding where to peck. Adaptation to environment has produced many defense mechanisms in animals—camouflage, speed, antlers—but in boobies it could only come up with a glare that humans might interpret as indignant outrage. Though on Seymour I did see a female—whistling, wings flapping—chase a sea lion away from her nest.

The word booby comes from the Spanish *bobo*, or clown. In the early days of sail, boobies would come sit on a hatch at the bow of ships, and from there they would fish. The hatch they chose came to be called—naturally—the booby hatch. (Even today if you get caught in a booby trap, you win the booby prize.) During courtship, blue-foots do a slow, high-stepping dance to show off their gaudy blue feet to each other.

As memorable as the boobies are the waved albatrosses of Isla Española, virtually the only place in the world they're found. Sam and I walked through their colony while several pairs were in the midst of their courtship ritual. It is an astounding show, a dance as intricate as Chinese acrobatics and as stylized as a Japanese dance-drama. A pair of the goose-size birds face off, then do a routine of bobbing and bowing, clicking and clattering, fencing and bill gaping, all the while grunting and chortling madly.

Awkward on land, albatrosses walk with a rolling, drunken-sailor gait. I watched one run a hundred yards over a boulder field, laboriously flapping its wings, trying to get airborne. It never got an inch off the ground and finally walked to a cliff overlooking the surf, leaned into the wind with wings spread, and soared confidently out to sea.

Standing on that same cliff edge, our guide Mike said, "And here is the most beautiful gull in the world." Gray and white, with a black head and a red eye ring, swallow-tailed gulls soared in the cold wind that howled over the cliff. To land, they faced into the wind, looked back over their shoulders, and settled gracefully onto narrow ledges—like someone backing a car into a garage. They have an endearing habit of standing and looking down at their feet, their heads bowed as if in prayer.

On beaches in the Galápagos, lava gulls—perhaps the rarest gull in the world—build solitary nests. We found one on Mosquera with four eggs in it, an unheard-of extravagance, for they always lay just two. But when we returned a few weeks later, the adults were gone and the eggs were shattered fragments. Probably sea lions had lumbered across them.

Offshore, fishing penguins float face down, like pieces of driftwood. Underwater, they swim like bullets, nearly too fast to follow. And brown noddies perch on the heads of pelicans, hoping for leftovers. Flightless cormorants, with pretty blue eyes, have here lost the need, and thus the ability, to fly. They nest near the water on lava boulders. We watched one repeatedly fetch mouthfuls of seaweed for its nesting mate, which growled and seemed gratified by the attention.

There are some unexpected birds in the Galápagos. Flamingos march in pink clouds back and forth across shallow lagoons, and mocking-birds, bold and aggressive, walk right up and sit on your toes. Many wear colored metal ankle bracelets, evidence of statistic-gathering ornithologists. Vermilion flycatchers and yellow warblers are the only colorful Galápagos land birds. The flycatchers dart through the air like bright red balls of fluff, their bills clicking audibly as they gather insects. At the hotel in Puerto Ayora, a warbler used an arbor as a lookout. From it, he would launch himself to catch moths, which he brought back to a sidewalk and dismantled with cool savagery.

Survival of the fittest is another concept Darwin expounded, and we saw it enacted on a bare coastal plain on Isla Genovesa. Thousands of storm petrels nest in cavities beneath the lava crust. Outside their burrows stand short-eared owls, waiting and waiting. We sat six feet from one of the owls and watched. It stood motionless at a burrow, occasionally glancing up at the petrels flying overhead. When it heard a sound from the burrow, it tensed like a cat and accidently kicked a pebble, making a slight noise. It looked up with a see-what-you-made-me-do expression, then settled down again. When the petrel finally emerged, the owl lunged, feet first, wings outspread. It stood on the struggling petrel, whose legs made feeble pedaling motions, dismembered it, and ate it.

It was on Genovesa that I found my favorite spot, a thin tidal estuary running parallel to the beach and separated from the sea by a wall of lava about 20 feet high. It was half a mile long, and it filled and emptied with the tides. Sit beside it for a couple of hours and here's what you see: A sea lion lazily fishing moseys up and back, then with a sudden spurt makes small fish jump in panic. Three mockingbirds stroll past, chirping a single note. Under a clump of mangroves, two lava gulls suddenly come to life. A third has landed in the lagoon, and the two dog-paddle out, murmuring warnings, and move the intruder on down the lagoon. When it flies off, they regroup, reassure each other, tug on opposite ends of a dead crab, then wash their bills and swim for home. A male frigatebird swoops down from above and, without landing, breaks off a dead branch from a shrub; he soars upward but drops the branch in the lagoon. He looks down at it, but doesn't try to retrieve it. The shadows of other frigates pass eerily overhead.

Behind me in the bushes are thousands of frigatebirds and boobies, many with chicks. Several male frigates are trying to attract females. They spread their wings, lean back, peer up into the sky, and inflate a red pouch, football-size, at their throats. It all looks as if big red flowers are blooming in the bushes. A frigatebird and a booby flit overhead, both shrieking, the frigate tugging on the booby's tail. A lava heron with a mean yellow eye walks along, staring down into the water as if looking in a mirror. In the sand at my feet, tiny fiddler crabs, like pebbles with feet, scuttle with jerky stops and starts. A red-footed booby behind me points upward with its bill, spreads its wings, and squawks and rattles as its mate arrives.

Nearby, two ruddy turnstones make the pebbles fly. A baby iguana beside me, barely six inches long, has the face of an ancient tortoise. An adult iguana walks down the beach, enters the water, swims across, climbs straight up a chunk of lava to the top, then turns to stone.

There remained one spectacle Sam and I had yet to see wild in the Galápagos—the giant tortoises, or *galápagos*, that gave the islands their name. On Isabela, each of the five volcanoes, separated by incredibly rough terrain, has its own subspecies of tortoise. They survive today on all of the volcanoes, most plentifully on Alcedo.

It was a hot and dusty climb to the rim of Alcedo. No delicate switchbacking for Galápagos trails; they go straight up the sides of the mountains. Alcedo's rim is a perfect doughnut, with a flat caldera in its middle. During the rainy season, ponds form there and the tortoises live around them. In the summer, the ponds dry up and the tortoises make the agonizing climb to the rim; there the huge clouds of garua that flow like water up from the sea and across the rim provide moisture until the rains return.

The mountaintop was crawling with hundreds of the mammoth reptiles. They inched through the underbrush like armored vehicles, following paths many centuries old. They look clumsy and accident-prone; you wonder how they can survive, yet surviving is what they do best. They may live 200 years. When startled, they withdraw into their shells, hissing as they expel air to make room for themselves. When you overtake and pass one on a trail, it hisses and withdraws, but by the time it gets itself tucked in, you're long gone; you feel as if you should apologize.

Buttoned up, the tortoises reminded me of hockey goalies, impenetrable and invulnerable, their padded knees folded across their faces. Each step they take seems to require a moment of thought, and when faced with an obstacle—a tent, say—their inclination is to go straight through it. Occasionally they get themselves seriously hung up. "Their crowning curse," Herman Melville wrote, "is their drudging impulse to straightforwardness in a belittered world."

We saw two males fighting. The battle seemed to take place in slow motion. One reached out and gradually nipped the other on the foot. The loser walked off rather quickly, evidently in headlong flight.

Old tortoises sometimes meet a poignant end. When they get too ancient and weak to feed themselves, they simply come to a stop. But the powers of endurance and the instinct to survive that have kept them alive for a century or more don't stop. So there they sit, perhaps for months, as the seasons turn and the cool garua washes across them, until finally the spark flickers and dies.

We camped a couple of nights on the rim of Alcedo, awakening to the forlorn braying of wild donkeys somewhere in the fog, and the songs of finches. By midmorning, clouds of garua would flow over us, but the clear night skies were etched by shooting stars—a fertile time for wishing. I let them pass. My wish—to see the Galápagos—had already been granted. As my Ecuadorian guide might have said: "I asked a desire, and it came true."

Boatbuilder Fritz Angermeyer relies on matazarno, *an island tree that yields durable wood for keels and hulls. About 10,000 people live in the Galápagos. They earn their living mainly by fishing,*

farming, or chartering boats to tourists. José Luis Gallardo (below, right) pets one of his Simmental cows, a Swiss breed. Some 14,000 head of cattle supply the islands with milk and beef.

FOLLOWING PAGES: *A prickly pear cactus grows as tall as a tree in the equatorial sunshine at Buccaneer Cove. The inlet's name recalls 16th-century freebooters who hid here after raiding Spanish ports.*

*R*are tool-user: A woodpecker finch (right) works a twig to pry a grub out of a tree branch. Of the 13 species of Galápagos finches, only the woodpecker and mangrove finches use tools. Gaudy showoff, a male frigatebird (below) attracts a mate by inflating a bright gular sac. Researcher Felipe Cruz (opposite) retrieves a dark-rumped petrel to check its banding, size, and weight. The bird's habit of nesting in burrows easily entered by pigs and rats now threatens the survival of this species.

DIETER AND MARY PLAGE (ABOVE)

A rock and a hard place cradle an abandoned egg, a blue-footed booby's. The nest nearby displays three eggs, the usual number laid by this species. In times of scarcity, the first chick to hatch monopolizes food, sentencing weaker nestlings to death by starvation. A lava lizard (below) warms itself on brain coral, exposed when tectonic uplift elevated the Isabela coastline.

*A land iguana surveys its volcanic
domain. Having an incredibly tough
mouth, these lizards can chew the fruits*

and pads of prickly pear cactus without
removing the sharp spines. On some
of the islands, introduced animals
endanger the once plentiful iguanas, so
Galápagos scientists breed them in
captivity for restocking natural habitats.

Sailor on a dolphin: Guide Mike Durban (opposite) stretches from the rigging to tickle a dolphin playing tag with the bow of Cachalote, a Galápagos charter boat. Above: Mike and his passengers hold their breath as Cachalote threads Kicker Rock, a narrow channel in an islet near San Cristóbal. In places, Galápagos waters amount to little more than a maze of rocks and reefs. Strong currents and high swells breaking against vertical sea cliffs, some of them 100 feet high, make coastal navigation dangerous.

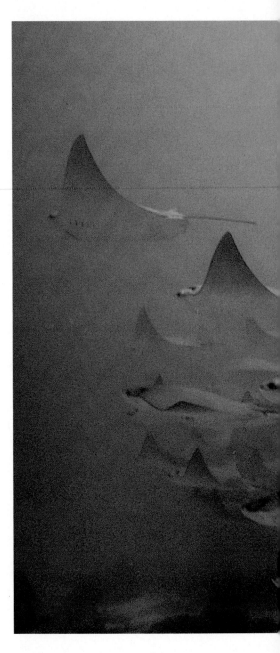

*G*olden rays (right) glide in formation near Roca Redonda, an offshore rock northwest of Isla Isabela. With undulating motion, the winglike fins propel the rays through the water, sometimes at great speeds. When threatened, they lash their enemy with their whiplike tails. A sea lion (above) surfs in roiling breakers. These creatures, the largest mammals in the Galápagos, seem always to be playing, whether with one another, marine iguanas, crabs, or just a piece of seaweed. Their antics have given them the reputation of being carefree clowns of the seas. All waters extending as far as 15 miles off the outer coasts of the Galápagos Islands lie within the Marine Resource Reserve; a plan currently under study by scientists and government officials would place part of the reserve within the Galápagos Islands National Park. Snorkelers and scuba divers tout the local waters as among the best for viewing an unusual diversity of fishes and sea plants.

*O*n the seafloor, a marine iguana clutches an algae-covered boulder. An English navigator called these nightmarish but harmless creatures "imps of darkness." The animal usually stays underwater for about ten minutes, but it can slow its heartbeat and settle in for as long as an hour. It eats algae, its blunt nose enabling it to crop the close-growing plants from the rocks. When mature, these reptiles—the only seagoing lizards in the world—average about three feet from snout to tail tip and weigh about five pounds. In breeding season, this dragon look-alike will try to intimidate his rivals by displaying the knobby spines and horns on his head. Found on most of the Galápagos Islands, marine iguanas often congregate in writhing piles to conserve body heat overnight. During the day they sun near the surf, sometimes as many as 5,000 sprawling along a mile of coast.

FOLLOWING PAGES: *A giant tortoise crawls along the rim of Alcedo Volcano in search of moisture blowing inland from the sea. From the Spanish word for these creatures—galápagos—comes the archipelago's familiar English name.*

JAPAN
Shores in the Shadow of Mountains

By Leslie Allen. Photographs by Scott Rutherford.

Modern and traditional architecture meet in Osaka, on Honshu, largest of Japan's islands. The sleek towers reflect the nation's economic rebirth; tree-edged Osaka Castle evokes a feudal past.

It may be the most famous garden in the world. But to most foreign visitors, the rock garden at the 15th-century temple called Ryoanji, in Japan's ancient capital of Kyoto, hardly looks like a garden at all. Its designer purposefully scattered 15 rocks of varied sizes and shapes around a large, level rectangle of raked gravel. From any vantage point at least one rock always, teasingly, remains out of sight. In this "dry landscape," as such Japanese gardens are called, the only hint of green is the thin layer of moss encircling the base of each rock.

There are dozens of other gardens in Kyoto, retreats offering eye-soothing lushness and the cool scent of pine as a balm to weary travelers. Yet as I begin my third trip to Japan, I seek out the austerity of the Ryoanji garden, as though on a private quest. As the morning mist lifts, I take in the sight from the wooden veranda of the Zen Buddhist temple to which the garden belongs. Viewers enter the garden not physically, but mentally; it was intended as an aid to meditation for those trying to attain the goal of Zen, *satori*, or spiritual enlightenment.

In this setting, a contemplative mood can creep up even on the uninitiated. Soon I leave behind my overwhelming image of Japan: the view from my airplane window of Tokyo, 230 miles to the east, a capital whose downtown spreads toward the horizon in all directions. In its own way, the garden at the Ryoanji also invites a loss of perspective, so that after a few minutes, this serene enclosure becomes a wild seascape. In my mind, the rippling sand is transformed into great swells, and the rocks become remote islands. Now my viewpoint changes: The rocks are majestic mountain peaks floating above thick clouds. This mix of imaginary land, sea, and mist seems both dewy with newness and as ancient as all the ages.

The garden at the Ryoanji is not meant to represent any single image in particular. We viewers each supply a personal meaning. I realize that I keep coming back to this place because, to me, it captures the traditions of Japan. On one level, I see the quiet spirit of Zen; on another, the Japanese reverence for simplicity, raised to an art. I marvel at the way tiny spaces are landscaped to evoke the grandeur of natural settings. But more than anything else, I see the essence of Japan, past and present, in the gravel and scattered rocks that bespeak the nation's island setting.

With a penchant for ordering, categorizing, and ranking, the Japanese once designated their nation's three most beautiful sights. All were island-studded vistas on Honshu: a potpourri of pine-clad islets on the northeast coast; Miya Jima, or Shrine Island, in the Inland Sea; and a sinuous sandbar and island in Wakasa Bay, off the Sea of Japan. In all, the archipelago, slightly smaller in land area than California, ranges more than 2,000 miles, from the Sea of Okhotsk off Siberia to the subtropical fringes of Taiwan. This sweep includes thousands of small islands and islets.

Japan's four largest islands—Honshu, Hokkaido, Kyushu, and Shikoku—are the vital core of the archipelago. With most of its people, and many of its major cities and industries and cultural centers such as Kyoto, Honshu forms the large midsection of dragon-shaped Japan. The country's mountainous spine rises to its most formidable heights here, where several peaks of the Japan Alps exceed 10,000 feet. Kyushu, the dragon's tail, also boasts bustling cities and highly industrialized areas in a setting of palm trees and citrus orchards. Its neighbor to the northeast, Shikoku, contains areas of industry in the north but has remained primarily rural in the south. The greatest contrast, though, is between urban Honshu and the sparsely populated setting of Hokkaido—the dragon's head. This island, the northernmost of Japan's major isles, is noted for dairy farms, vast forests, and large crater lakes, along with some industry.

Despite the contrasts, Japan's mountains and coastlines form a continuous tapestry of scenic beauty. No place in the nation is more than 93 miles from the sea. Gentle forested slopes, in one location, frame a rugged, wave-lashed promontory; in another place, sunbathers on a creamy beach gaze up at a smoldering volcano. On a world map, the surrounding seas define Japan's four main islands as a tidy unit. About 120 miles of the Korea Strait—six times the width of the English Channel—separate Japan from mainland Asia to the west.

Practically from the moment I arrive, I never stop seeing how geography has influenced the Japanese. In the airport, I watch corporate managers, back from abroad, and think of Japan's lack of raw materials and its dependence on imports as reasons for its need to be powerful in the international marketplace. I delight in the politeness that I am accorded and think of the traditional need for civility in a crowded land: Japan is one twenty-fifth the size of the United States but has a population about half that of the U.S. When schoolchildren in Tokyo stop and stare wide-eyed at me, a foreigner, I think of feudal Japan, whose leaders took advantage of its island status to isolate it from the world for more than two centuries.

My quest for the uniqueness of island Japan comes into clearest focus, however, on the smaller isles and on the more remote coastlines of the larger ones. There the water still endows tradition; the shifting scenes of sand and sea, crag and coast, remain unmarred; there I can taste and touch island Japan.

At Sakurajima—formerly an island—near the southern tip of Kyushu, I receive a bone-numbing lesson in the origin of all of Japan's islands from Ishi Nakashima, a 63-year-old farm woman who skillfully balances a sheaf of newly cut rice straw and a glinting scythe on her head. She has lived for the past 40 years about a mile from the crater of an active volcano. Moreover, this is the most active of more than 60 active volcanoes throughout Japan, one of the earth's most geologically unstable regions. It has erupted many times since A.D. 708; in 1914, it disgorged about four billion tons of lava that joined Sakurajima to the Kyushu mainland. Since the mid-1950s, volcanic activity has been picking up again.

What "activity" means right now is that the dense billow of white smoke rising from the crater turns black as we watch. At the same time, the noise coming from the crater, a distant swoosh a moment ago, begins to approximate the rumble of a 747's take-off roll. The ground seems to quake, and I fight an impulse to run away. Terrifying! Not to Mrs. Nakashima, though. Real fright to her takes the shape of fiery two-ton boulders that have occasionally catapulted out of the crater and down the mountainside. Smaller ones pose a danger too.

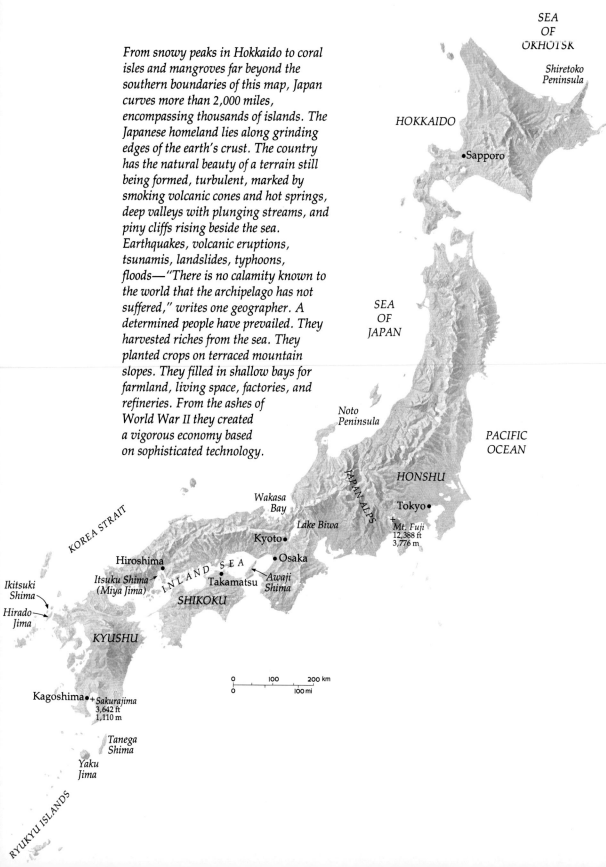

JAPAN

From snowy peaks in Hokkaido to coral
isles and mangroves far beyond the
southern boundaries of this map, Japan
curves more than 2,000 miles,
encompassing thousands of islands. The
Japanese homeland lies along grinding
edges of the earth's crust. The country
has the natural beauty of a terrain still
being formed, turbulent, marked by
smoking volcanic cones and hot springs,
deep valleys with plunging streams, and
piny cliffs rising beside the sea.
Earthquakes, volcanic eruptions,
tsunamis, landslides, typhoons,
floods—"There is no calamity known to
the world that the archipelago has not
suffered," writes one geographer. A
determined people have prevailed. They
harvested riches from the sea. They
planted crops on terraced mountain
slopes. They filled in shallow bays for
farmland, living space, factories, and
refineries. From the ashes of
World War II they created
a vigorous economy based
on sophisticated technology.

SEA
OF
ORHOTSK

Shiretoko
Peninsula

HOKKAIDO

•Sapporo

SEA
OF
JAPAN

Noto
Peninsula

PACIFIC
OCEAN

JAPAN ALPS

HONSHU

Tokyo•

Wakasa
Bay

Lake Biwa

+
Mt. Fuji
12,388 ft
3,776 m

Kyoto•

•Osaka

KOREA STRAIT

Hiroshima

INLAND SEA

Takamatsu

Awaji
Shima

Itsuku Shima
(Miya Jima)

SHIKOKU

Ikitsuki
Shima

Hirado
Jima

KYUSHU

0   100   200 km
0   100 mi

Kagoshima•• +Sakurajima
3,642 ft
1,110 m

Tanega
Shima

Yaku
Jima

RYUKYU ISLANDS

"If those rocks hit your house, it burns right down. And when it rains, all those rocks just float like bean curd in the river," she says. "This used to be a very nice place. We'd harvest a lot of tangerines and plums, and other things to sell to Tokyo, but now there's no real harvest because of the ash and gas. Just look at my field." Indeed, the ground is the color of gunmetal, and the eggplants that Mrs. Nakashima has just picked are puny specimens. She has finally accepted the government's offer to relocate her and her family. They will move to the city.

Why didn't she leave sooner? Her land was blighted, her safety imperiled. For one thing, she was reluctant, as are many Japanese, to leave behind an ancestral home. For another, her choices for a new homesite were few because of the high demand for living space. In most habitable parts of this mountainous country, every scrap of level or rolling land is put to use. Crowding is the accepted norm. That's not to say that seclusion can't be found. It just requires a bit of wandering off the beaten trail.

To me, Yaku Jima takes the prize as a solitude-lover's retreat. I decide to visit the pearl-shaped island because Japanese friends have told me of its drama and beauty. Other places in Japan, they say, looked like Yaku Jima before they were developed. As you approach by prop plane from mainland Kyushu, a 40-minute ride from the north, Yaku Jima wells up from the sea with eerie suddenness. Your plane, swooping in for a landing, is a fly buzzing amid natural skyscrapers: What Yaku Jima lacks in breadth, a mere 16 miles, it gains in height. Mount Miyanoura, rising 6,349 feet above the Pacific, dominates the isle's cluster of peaks. Almost all of the island is a national parkland, a preserve of 46,301 acres of crystalline streams, waterfalls, hot springs, orchids, rhododendrons. Plentiful rainfall nurtures the luxuriance. What appears to be missing is the people.

"We have 20,000 people, 20,000 monkeys, and 20,000 deer," boast the airport vendors. Soon, in your rental car, it is easy to start counting. Brief white flashes signal the deer skittering off the road ahead. When the going gets a bit rougher, on the rutted mud track that switchbacks through the forest, Yaku's red-faced monkeys, *Yakuzaru,* swing out of trees and shyly watch your progress. You can total up the deer and monkeys, it seems, before the human numbers start adding up.

But the airport vendors have neglected to mention the greatest of all of Yaku Jima's attractions, the thousands of great cedars that grow here. Some are 55 feet in girth and more than 130 feet tall. Those that are at least a thousand years old are called *Yakusugi.* Anything younger is called a *Yakukosugi,* a "small" cedar. These trees leave you speechless, but not in the way California's redwoods do, racing the eye upward to where a sunbeam glints through distant needles. Japan's cedars are not streamlined, but deeply furrowed and knotted, with cabin-size trunks and with smaller trees, vines, and other plants growing out of their limbs. At the base of one hoary cedar, there is a tiny shrine. In Shinto, Japan's native religion, the *kami,* or spirits, include the wonders of nature.

Harmony with the natural world is a touchstone of traditional Japanese culture, and the image of ideal nature a tame and comforting one. It is the gentle curve of a snow-laden branch, the restful symmetry of Japan's most revered landmark—Mount Fuji—or a soft profusion of pink cherry blossoms, not dark wildernesses that resound with the cries of unknown beasts. Where nature displays a wilder side, as in Yaku Jima, it lures people who crave awe. Conspicuous among them are artists—Hiroyuki and Mika Yoshitoshi, for instance, young potters from Tokyo. In Hiroyuki's studio hang posters that advertise his one-man shows in chic Tokyo galleries. He says he has come for the "direct experience" that Yaku Jima offers.

"I don't want smooth, beautiful surfaces, but hard ones," he tells me. "There is a lot of sand, and stones, in my clay." One of his works, a charcoal-colored pitcher with a shimmer of iron, is as much a tactile as a visual delight. It feels cool and grainy, like beach sand underfoot where the tide has just receded. Another source of inspiration for Hiroyuki is Yaku Jima's "many special plants and different kinds of wood," which he burns in his kiln. He shows me the results in his pottery: A mustard tone comes from ash, while pine yields a different yellow, and oak and cedar produce contrasting shades of green. He will sometimes burn different woods, grasses, and minerals together to get a mix of tones as subtle as the muted colors of Yaku Jima itself.

The island could be considered a rarity in modern Japan, a blank canvas where the acts of man appear as bold as a calligrapher's fat black brushstrokes. The ambivalence of its people about the approaches of the outside world, though, reflects a deep current in Japan's history.

The first recorded arrival of Westerners took place on Tanega Shima, about 12 miles east of Yaku Jima, in the early 1540s. The newcomers were Portuguese traders from a Chinese junk blown off course. Though paired by proximity, long flat Tanega Shima—people say—resembles a musket, and rounded Yaku Jima a cannonball. The comparisons are meaningful: It was the Portuguese who introduced firearms to Japan.

Soon thereafter, various local leaders granted the Portuguese trading rights and let Roman Catholic missionaries try to win converts. Trade with the West expanded, the Spanish coming to Nagasaki on the western coast of Kyushu and the Dutch and English establishing themselves on Hirado, an island northwest of Nagasaki. In this region, as well as throughout much of Japan, Christianity took root.

But in the Japanese converts and in the foreign missionaries who taught them, Japan's leaders began to see a threat of disloyalty and even subversion. Beginning in the late 16th century, they issued a series of edicts that banned Christianity in their country. The restrictions remained in force for about 250 years. During this time thousands of Roman Catholics were put to death. Yet pockets of Christianity survived in some places, among them the islands off northwestern Kyushu.

Boarding a ferryboat, I set out for one such "Christian island." There are so many small islands sprinkled across the water that, at the ferry's railing, I must squint hard to distinguish the distant ones from whitecaps on this blustery day. In this constantly shifting scene, sheer cliffs seem to part like stage curtains, revealing pine-clad crags or a tiny cove of startling sapphire blue. What had seemed far is now close; what was close slips off to the distance. But finally I'm on terra firma on Ikitsuki Shima, standing there in broad daylight, holding two enormous bottles of *sake,* or rice wine. The sake will figure in a matter of great seriousness, the ceremonies of a Christian group here. They are descendants of the *kakure Kirishitan,* or hidden Christians, who for two and a half centuries practiced their faith in secret. Some Japanese Christians still follow the old rituals, and today I have been invited to join them.

As I ride toward a hilltop farmhouse, the car windows frame persimmon trees laden with ripe, orange-colored fruit. I am apprehensive because only a few outsiders have ever been allowed to attend this ceremony. But the celebrants, three farmers, greet me with smiles, deep bows, and cups of tea. They place the sake into a niche of a small altar amid flickering candles, explaining that in the days when Christianity was a capital offense, the sacramental sake served to disguise prayer meetings as parties.

I notice a little Buddhist altar in an adjoining room. "We are Christian *and* Buddhist," explains Hayakichi Masuyama, one of my hosts. "The reason our ancestors practiced Buddhism was to hide their Christianity. Everyone belonged to a Buddhist temple." A small, delicate porcelain statue, with babe in arms, could be a Buddhist goddess of mercy, or the Virgin Mary; a tiny inconspicuous cross was carved into one foot.

In days past, if a zealous government official discovered written religious materials in a home it might be the first step toward a death sentence. "I learned all of the ceremonies orally. Word by word, it took about 40 days, several hours a day, with my teacher," says Sakichi Deguchi, a wizened gentleman of 83. With few written works and no priests to guide them, the Christians developed, over generations, their own ritual of chanting and prayer. They called it *orashio,* from the Latin word for speech, *oratio.* We kneel Japanese style on *tatami,* or straw mats, around a low table, and the men pray aloud in unison. Over the centuries of hiding, the words have become a garbled mix of Japanese, Latin, and Portuguese that many of the Japanese Christians understand poorly. I begin to feel slightly lost in place as well as time.

But then: "*Santa Maria . . . Santo Paulo . . . Espírito Santo. . . .*" On this island in a foreign land, an ancient, alien ritual begins to come full circle toward familiarity as I make out these chanted words.

In the late 19th century when the religious ban was lifted, some of the hidden Christians living in this area publicly rejoined the Catholic church. Like their forebears, my hosts chose not to. Why?

"After so many generations," says Shigeru Hashimoto, "it has just become a natural thing." There is also an unwillingness to relinquish the remembrance of their ancestors' tribulations.

Nowadays, life on the island is calm. People move about at a relaxed pace. Old fishing boats at anchor fly gay banners for a holiday, and rack upon rack of drying fish make the air pungent. The only thing that suggests modern Japan is the blare of the television baseball announcer as the Seibu Lions and the Hanshin Tigers move into the 13th inning.

The game is still tied up about 20 minutes later when our ferry reaches the island of Hirado, just off Kyushu. Here ruddy bluffs alternate with vibrant green rice fields, and subtropical flora thrives along with Japanese cherry trees, azaleas, and bamboos. A whitewashed Catholic church can whisk the imagination off to other lands. What almost defies the imagination is the fact that more than three and a half centuries ago foreign trade flourished in what is today the quiet port of Hirado. There are a few clues. The stone quay, on which a lone fisherman is dozing, was built by the Dutch; here their ships busily unloaded spices, watches, eyeglasses, and took aboard porcelain, gold objects, silver coins.

One well-known European closely associated with Hirado was Will Adams—the English navigator who became an adviser to Japan's ruler in the 1600s. The character John Blackthorne in the novel *Shogun* is loosely modeled on Adams, who is memorialized on a stone tablet in a hillside park. But the sight that dominates the town is its great white hillside castle, a symbol of the Matsuura family, whose rule of this isle and parts of Kyushu dates back to the 13th century. In the early 17th, it was the ruling Matsuuras who supported the efforts of the Dutch and English traders on the island.

The feudal system ended more than a century ago, but the Matsuura family name is still respected in Hirado. The family believes that its line stretches so far back that an early Matsuura was the model for a Japanese mythological figure. Nevertheless, bespectacled Tadashi Matsuura, representing the 41st generation of his family, is decidedly down-to-earth. We are in his Western-style home, flanked by an ancient teahouse, gardens, and ponds on the castle grounds; the castle itself is now open to the public. His wife, Yoriko, is serving green tea and translucent pastel sweets.

Tadashi Matsuura appears modest even among the normally self-effacing Japanese, and he pauses a bit when asked about his family's accomplishments. "We participated in early trade with foreign countries," he explains, "and receiving culture and learning from Europe helped Japan to advance. My family was not the most powerful among Japan's *daimyo*. Our domain was big, but much of it was wild and uncultivated. Still, it seems we were well-off because we had seafood, and whales, and salt from China.

"Because we did have money, the lords Matsuura didn't have to force the farmers to pay heavy taxes—in those days, people paid with rice. They trusted the lord because he treated them well. He had many responsibilities. He saw that roads, buildings, and schools were built, and land reclaimed. He was also the court of law."

What does it mean, I wonder, to be a Matsuura today?

For Tadashi Matsuura, as for his forebears, it has meant leadership. He was an elected assemblyman for more than two decades and later became head of the local education commission. Now, from retirement, he measures the changes of the 20th century against the ancient continuity and stability of his family and the community it ruled.

One likely change strikes a personal note. As Yoriko Matsuura says: "I'm afraid that none of our children will return to live here." The 42nd generation of the family includes three grown children in Tokyo, and one elsewhere on Kyushu. "It's important for at least one of them to live here. But there's a problem, and that is that there wouldn't be any jobs for them here." They're all skilled professionals. "I think," she says, "that while they work they should stay in Tokyo, and maybe return after retirement." The dilemma is not unique to the Matsuuras. Since Hirado's brief involvement with overseas trade centuries ago, prosperity has eluded it, and many islanders have left to work elsewhere. But now to many Hirado residents, their island has a new symbol of promise. To see it on cloth paintings sold elsewhere on Kyushu makes you think that people in this part of Japan have an odd fascination with San Francisco's Golden Gate Bridge. In fact, since 1977, the great steel-and-concrete structure resembling the famed American landmark has spanned the channel that isolated Hirado from Kyushu. So far, the bridge has brought a moderate increase in tourism, but most people say that it is too early to predict its lasting effects on the island.

By allowing the 17th-century Dutch and English to set up trading posts at Hirado, the Matsuuras helped make the island a bridge between Japan and the world. Today, Tadashi Matsuura claims that when he was Hirado's assemblyman in the early 1970s, he lobbied neither for nor against the bridge. Nevertheless, he reveals his devotion to his family's traditional ideals: "A place like Japan itself, and especially a place like Hirado," he says, "is, foremost, an island. People who live on islands often have a kind of spirit, or mentality, that is narrow-minded. So I think that it's a good idea to have a bridge here because it will change that. And as time goes by, I can already see that narrow-minded mentality fading here."

Japan may be a nation fragmented by water, but it is also the land of Toyota and Nissan, a nation increasingly enamored of the automobile. Though hundreds of ferries ply coastal waters, an ever growing network of highways offers alternative means of travel to most destinations. At the time of my visit, construction neared completion on a 33.5-mile tunnel—the world's longest—to link Honshu and Hokkaido. Mammoth bridges, some of them still unfinished, span the Inland Sea, the large body of water enclosed by Shikoku, Kyushu, and southern Honshu. The most ambitious is the Seto Ohashi, Great Bridge of the Inland Sea—in fact a complex of 11 bridges, which will hopscotch its way 5.8 miles across five small islands. An upper deck will hold an expressway for motor traffic; a lower level will accommodate trains. It will be the largest such bridge system in the world, its builders say.

On Awaji, the Inland Sea's largest island, I am surprised to discover how a new bridge has affected a centuries-old local tradition, the Awaji puppet theater. Attending a performance, a sad play, I'm intrigued by the narrator's voice spiraling into a high-pitched plaint to the accompanying strains of a *samisen*. The detailed costumes of the stringless, almost life-size puppets entrance me, as do the incredibly subtle movements of the black-hooded puppeteers who stand behind the puppets and manipulate them.

The Awaji puppet theater is known throughout Japan as part of the nation's great cultural heritage. After World War II, according to Masaru Umazume, the director of the theater, movies and television almost killed it. Puppeteers and audiences became scarce. But as the country recovered from the war and tourism increased, the theater found new energy. Now the bridge is helping to give the theater a vital boost. The parking lot is filled with cars and tour buses, and extra performances have been added.

On other, smaller Inland Sea islands, the bridges promise truly disruptive change. One such place is Yo Shima. Home to some 300 inhabitants, it is merely a high mound that can be crossed in half an hour on foot. Now a high pylon for the Seto Ohashi Bridge overwhelms one end of the island. Construction required that dozens of homes be torn down. The elementary school, perched on a hillside, is near the bridge; children will hear cars and trains streaking by every day. After centuries of relative isolation, change will surely seem sudden. Yet most island residents look forward to the bridge because it will facilitate basic services such as mail delivery.

One resident points out that bridge construction at sites around the Inland Sea has turned up many treasures for archaeology. The artifacts indicate that for centuries this body of water has been a major trade route as well as a cultural crossroads. Yet today, the Inland Sea, in some ways, is viewed as an obstacle to transportation and development.

Nevertheless, oceans near and far are one of Japan's most important natural resources, providing an amazingly varied bounty of seafood. I fancy myself a seafood connoisseur, but I never dreamed that in Japan I would savor half a dozen new varieties of crab, or clams ranging in size from a thumbnail to a large man's fist.

In places, where tides and currents permit, the sea is now farmed as intensively as level land. Oysters and scallops are raised beneath offshore rafts. In the Japanese way, nothing is done halfheartedly. Musical sounds broadcast from radio towers to underwater speakers lure fish that, like Pavlov's dogs, have been trained to associate sound with food. Sea bream, in particular, rise to the bait of soft tones.

Alongside high technology, deeply traditional relationships of people with the sea survive. These bonds include livelihoods passed from father to son and, occasionally, from mother to daughter. Only a few women in Japan work on the water, and—along with some men—only a fraction of these still follow the old, arduous ways of the *ama*, or diver for shellfish.

I encounter a few female ama getting ready for work early one brilliant Sunday morning on the Noto Peninsula, on the Japan Sea coast of Honshu. In their vans by the side of the road, they slouch out of sight to wriggle into their wet suits—concessions to modern times. Traditionally, their mothers wore practically nothing at all to dive for abalone, sea cucumber, and other marine delicacies. Otherwise, little about their diving techniques has changed.

Today, they ride for several miles along the squiggly coast road to a sheltered cove inside a breakwater. I follow them, down a steep gravel track to the water's edge. Quickly and silently, the women make their preparations to dive. Black inner tubes hurled from the van hit the ground: thump, thump, thump. Into netting attached to the tubes' inner rims go little plastic bags. "Those hold our lunch, pudding and juice," says a rosy-cheeked young ama who, instead of diving today, is acting as the group's chauffeur. "We rest between dives, holding onto our inner tubes, and sipping and eating a bit." Ama go into the water before 9 a.m., she says, and usually don't end their day until midafternoon. "The newer ama come back exhausted, but once you get used to it, it's all right." Some of these women are in their 50s and 60s.

The divers put on their flippers. They are now in black from head to toe. Sleek as seals, they are off into a deep blue choppy sea, pushing their inner tubes before them as they swim out. When they reach their destination about half a mile from the shore, all I can see are the tiny splashes of dives and, after seemingly endless intervals, the bobbing of heads. In her prime, an ama can dive 30 times an hour to a depth of 40 feet to grab abalone off the seafloor.

Every generation of women in her family up to herself, says the ama at my side—reluctant to give her name—has included divers. "I only got as far as junior high school," she says, "and I couldn't find another job, so I had to be an ama. I didn't like it then, but I do now." The work, though tiring, isn't really dangerous, she says, and it's "a profitable way for a woman to make a living."

The meat of the abalone, prized throughout Japan, commands princely sums; delicate *sazae*, a kind of sea snail, plucked offshore by the ama, also carries a high market value. The skills of the ama, she says, come naturally to girls who can swim almost like mermaids at an early age. Traditionally, many of them learned to dive during the golden days of summer. Motioning toward small islands barely visible on the horizon, she smiles wistfully. "My mother had a summer house out there. With the water all around them, young girls just naturally learned how to be divers."

To many Japanese the small offshore islands and coastal backwaters bypassed by explosive postwar development seem havens of a bygone lifeway. This is literally true for a few thousand Japanese who left their homes on the southern Kurils when the Soviet Union occupied these islands at the end of World War II. The Kurils are remote, strung out just beyond northeastern Hokkaido—itself a remote land of dark forests, purply marsh, and windblown beaches. Snow often blankets the roads here by October's end. Three weeks earlier, however, the brief, intense blush of a northern fall rivals the autumn scenery of New England, at the same latitude.

Along parts of the northeastern coast are small fishing villages where many former Kuril residents now live. On clear days the outlines of some of the Kurils can be seen from the villages. It is then that the longing for childhood homes becomes most intense.

"We had everything we wanted," reminisces one man. "It was a perfect garden. It was a complete balance of sea and rivers and mountains and harbors. The winters were mild. And we even rode wild horses on the cliffs above the sea."

His nostalgia is directed at a speck in the Pacific called Shikotan. His voice resonates across a vastness of time and space, though. It calls forth not one island, but an ancient and powerful ideal of harmony, born with the notion of Japan itself.

Abandoned by its mother, a red fox cub finds safety in the arms of a young friend, Koruri Taketazu. She lives in rural Hokkaido, the northernmost of Japan's main islands. The Japanese once considered the fox a magic creature. They believed that the gods would punish anyone who killed the animal. Today, foxes, deer, even bears, still find wild refuges on Hokkaido, regarded as Japan's last frontier. A visitor (opposite) strolls near the hot spring at Iwaobetsu on Hokkaido's Shiretoko Peninsula. His padded kimono, called a tanzen, *wards off the autumn chill. Hokkaido's national parks offer rocky sea coasts, dense primeval forests, deep crater lakes, steaming volcanic peaks. Fertile fields of rice and vegetables cover much of the island's level land. Cattle and horses graze in high-walled valleys. Factories producing wood pulp, iron, and steel cluster south of Sapporo, the island's capital and largest city.*

MICHAEL S. YAMASHITA (ABOVE)

Laughter lights the faces of two schoolgirls on Honshu sharing fruit slices after class on Saturday. Like all Japanese schoolchildren, they attend class five and a half days a week. The color of the identical hats that the girls are wearing identifies their grade level. Hats of a single color help teachers keep an eye on youngsters during field trips.

For everyday wear, sneakers and rubber boots have replaced straw sandals and wooden clogs. Outdoor shoes (opposite) line shelves near the entryway of a nursery school. In class, students wear soft shoes made for the indoors. At left, a morning-glory vine, used in the study of natural science, twines past the window of a preschool classroom.

Unorthodox footwear clashes with a seven-year-old's ceremonial kimono. Zori, similar to those on her mother's feet, will complete the traditional costume. Opposite: Two geisha visit a park in Takamatsu on Shikoku. Skilled singers and dancers, geisha help keep the ancient arts of Japan alive.

*L*andscape art: Twisted maples, a
secluded pond, and more than 120 kinds
of mosses adorn Kyoto's Saihoji, or Moss
Temple. Its lake garden, laid out by
Buddhists in the 12th century A.D. and
reshaped 150 years later, still offers
earthly reflections of the heavenly
paradise of Buddha's disciple Amida.
The landscaping conforms to the
Japanese ideal of bringing balance and
harmony to nature in its raw state. A
bamboo dipper (opposite) rests on the
stone basin in another garden. Far right:
Ornamental koi, or carp, flash in an
azalea-edged pond. In a nation crowded
with people, gardens set aside for quiet
meditation or for the appreciation of
beauty provide welcome retreats.

67

bstract scenery: A Zen Buddhist garden in Kyoto features a mound of moss and stones of varying shapes and sizes that symbolize longevity. "Dry landscapes," such as this garden, stir the imagination and aid in meditation. Rocks become islands and mountains; gravel, a sea. The monk below rakes gravel into concentric circles, symbols of ocean waves and, in a broader sense, the enlightenment of Zen. Garden experts note the spell of such havens: "What . . . seems like a simple sandbox becomes a garden . . . an entire universe without bounds."

FOLLOWING PAGES: The sea wind teases rock-bound pines. Japan's jagged coastline and myriad small islets have inspired austere temple gardens as well as poems, ink-wash pictures, and vivid screen paintings.

"*Cleanliness and purity*," says Hiroshi Kamisugi, "*are basic to Shinto.*" Immaculately clad in robes attesting to that tenet, he serves as the hundredth head priest at the Kamisugi Izumuhime Shrine on Honshu's Noto Peninsula. The wooden tablet he holds dates from A.D. 1320 and tells the story of the rebuilding of the shrine at that time. Many Japanese practice both Shinto, Japan's indigenous religion, and Buddhism, introduced in the sixth century A.D. From Buddhism they derive their beliefs about an afterlife.

To Shinto they owe their reverence for nature. In Shinto "there is no place where a god does not reside," one observer says. Spirits, or kami, inhabit the animate and inanimate alike: the wind, the moon, a tree, even an island—such as Itsuku Shima (below), also called Miya Jima, or Shrine Island. A torii, or Shinto gate, graces Hiroshima Bay and forms a ceremonial entrance to the Itsuku Shima Shrine; it honors three daughters of the ocean god Susanoo. Japanese consider this hallowed island one of their nation's loveliest sights.

*A*sh-laden smoke pours from the southern peak of Sakurajima, not far from the southern tip of Kyushu. This volcano, Japan's most active, has erupted scores of times since its first recorded outburst in A.D. 708. Recent activity ruined fruit and vegetable crops at the base of the cone and forced nearby residents to leave. Across the bay, Kagoshima (opposite)—a city of half a million—rests uneasily in the shadow of the mountain. People fend off raining ash with umbrellas, and daily weather reports tell wind patterns so that local residents know when it is safe to hang out their laundry. Ages ago movement of the Pacific tectonic plate gave rise to volcanoes that helped produce the spectacular mountain scenery of this archipelago off the Asian mainland.

FOLLOWING PAGES: Snow dusts the moated grounds of Tokyo's Imperial Palace, home of Japan's emperor.

75

IRELAND
Stronghold of a Storied Past

By Thomas O'Neill. Photographs by Michael S. Yamashita.

On the North Atlantic coast, a thatched
cottage preserves the flavor of old
Ireland. A moist climate warmed by the
Gulf Stream flowing just offshore brings
lushness to the fields of the Emerald Isle.

The Irish call them "soft days"—those times when mist hangs like a veil over the countryside, gently blurring field and village. Nobody bothers much about the drizzle: Pale skies and a spray of rain are as much a feature of Irish life as Sunday Mass, a herd of cows stopping traffic on a country lane, or pints of stout gleaming darkly in a smoky pub. "It's moist enough in places," an Irishman told me, "that throw an old boot out in the yard in autumn, by spring it will be covered with moss."

Praise then the soft days for giving us the green mantle of Ireland— the velvety fields divided by hedgerows and beloved of milk cow and racehorse, lawns as smooth and bright as the felt on a billiard table, the mountainsides wearing thick pelts of grass. Famous are the green acres of Ireland, born of rain and lime soil, deep-hued and pastoral. The Emerald Isle it is.

Given the seductive beauty of Ireland's plush vistas, my mind, long after I've returned from visiting the island, keeps returning to *stones*. I see images of gray, coarse, embedded stones—as if shafts of light fell on them out of the pewter sky. I see field boulders luminous in the milky northern light, scattered about by long-ago glaciers. I see broad, worn stones, arranged in circles atop mountains deemed sacred by inhabitants thousands of years before. I see stones piled up to make fences for isolated farms, and I see massive cut stones that crumbled from a medieval castle. I remember the stones I carried, according to custom, to the top of Knocknarea Mountain to the burial cairn of Queen Maeve, the warrior queen who lived in Celtic mythology. And I can still feel the stone in a graveyard in County Wicklow where I traced with my fingers the name of Patrick O'Neill, my great-great-grandfather.

These stones, in all their shapes and forms, are the bones of Ireland's past. They haunt the landscape, serving as mute codes of invasion and worship, of kinship and myth, of continuity and permanence. The rocky, verdant countryside of Ireland is drenched in history: Celtic kings and Viking marauders, Norman knights and English gentry, Scottish settlers and Irish patriots have all left marks. Their settlements and their monuments have helped confer on this isle at the edge of Europe a potency and vividness of culture that grips the imagination of the Western world.

The ghosts of Ireland's past do not reveal themselves only in ruins and ancient-looking landscapes; the past thrives as a warm-blooded presence in the lives of the Irish people as well. A swirl of memory and folktale, of superstition and custom, regularly colors the Irish sense of their surroundings. Why were so many prehistoric earthworks, such as burial mounds and hill forts, left undisturbed? Because farmers to this day believe that fairies—Irish spirits—may inhabit them.

For farmer Tom Byrne, who tends cattle on a shaggy pasture overlooking the Atlantic Ocean, home ground amounts to a scroll of handed-down tales. He lives on the Burren, an eerie rock-encrusted plateau that rises in the northwest corner of County Clare on Ireland's rugged west coast. On an exotic sunstruck morning in early autumn, Tom invited me to join him on a walk to the pasture on the mountain behind his house. He needed to check his one hundred head of cattle, he said. His collie flashed ahead of us, through fern and heather, as the sturdy farmer and I mounted the steep slope. In a rolling brogue, he told me how the old IRA (Irish Republican Army) had hidden in the Burren hinterlands from British troops during the guerrilla war of independence in 1919-1920. He pointed out the gaunt outlines of an old potato bed lying near collapsed stone foundations and recalled the fate of Aghaglinny. Residents had to abandon this village during the Great Famine of the 1840s. The pestilence came in the form of a potato blight that devastated the one-crop economy of Ireland and left death and emigration in its wake.

One story stuck with me more than the rest. It captured the imagination and awe that the Irish invest in their environment. "See Gleninagh Castle," Tom said, aiming his walking stick at the ruins of a watchtower on the coastline below us. "An English landlord owned a big house next to it. There's a tale that this hard landlord once brought up water from the sacred well at a nearby church, and it wouldn't boil for him—a sign that he was evil. There was an eel swimming in the water. The landlord knew his Irish tenants believed that if they saw an eel in the water, the water could cure their aches and pains. So he cruelly chopped the eel in three. And do you know that the next time he went back to the well, the eel was there in one piece with two scars on its back?"

The Irish tell such stories with sincerity and nonchalance, quietly daring you to disbelieve them. Probably ever since nomadic fishermen and hunters came to Ireland's shores in the Middle Stone Age, some 8,000 years ago, the scenery has been charged with mysticism and drama. Hilltops especially became wreathed with significance. Many of them came to feature prominent tombs, royal forts, or annual assembly grounds.

Some hilltops have long remained sacred, such as Croagh Patrick, a stony, 2,510-foot pinnacle looking down on Clew Bay in County Mayo. For centuries, pagan Celts celebrated the harvest festival of Lughnasa on its summit. In the fifth century A.D., St. Patrick—the former slave who led the movement to convert Ireland to Christianity—reputedly spent 40 days praying and fasting on the mountain. Legend says it is from here that St. Patrick drove into the sea the snakes plaguing Ireland. Truth be told, the offending serpents were symbols of pagan sexuality condemned by the Catholic church. Actual snakes have never been present in Ireland. Today the mountain preserves its holy attraction. On the last Sunday of July, the same time as the ancient Celtic holiday, thousands of Catholic pilgrims—some barefoot—ascend Croagh Patrick to do penance and hear Mass.

Ireland usually surprises the first-time visitor with the extent of its highlands. The island has been likened to a saucer: flat in the middle, raised on the rim. Mountain ranges and cliffs rise like stormy waves around much of the island's perimeter. Their names are tongue-pleasing: Slieve League, Knockmealdown, MacGillicuddy's Reeks, Glanaruddery. Sometimes the mountains thrust into the sea and create fjordlike bays and lofty peninsulas, as in the scenic coastal region of County Kerry in southwestern Ireland.

Along the ragged Atlantic coastline brush the warm currents of the Gulf Stream, helping keep the island's climate tame. The weather remains mild and moist year-round, with roses blooming well into autumn on the Galway coast. Ireland is roughly the size of Maine, and no point on the

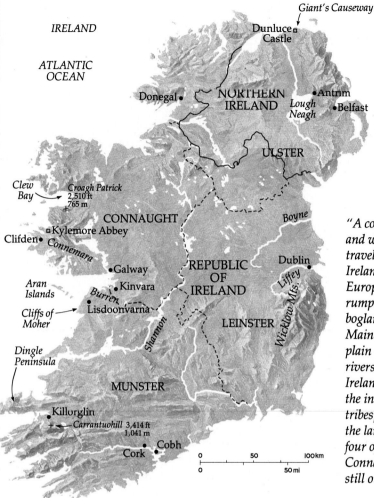

IRELAND

ATLANTIC
OCEAN

Giant's Causeway

Dunluce
Castle

Donegal •

NORTHERN
IRELAND

Lough
Neagh

• Antrim
• Belfast

IRISH
SEA

ULSTER

Clew
Bay

Croagh Patrick
2,510 ft
765 m

CONNAUGHT

□ Kylemore Abbey

Clifden • Connemara

• Galway

Aran
Islands

Burren • Kinvara

Cliffs of
Moher

Lisdoonvarna

Dingle
Peninsula

MUNSTER

• Killorglin

+ Carrantuohill 3,414 ft
1,041 m

Cork

Cobh

Boyne

REPUBLIC
OF
IRELAND

Dublin •

Liffey

LEINSTER

Wicklow Mts.

Shannon

0   50   100 km

0   50 mi

*"A country of uneven surface . . . soft
and watery": A 12th-century Welsh
traveler thus accurately described
Ireland, the westernmost island of the
European continental shelf. Mountains
rumple the island's perimeter. Mossy
bogland blankets nearly one-fifth of the
Maine-size area. Even the fertile central
plain dips and rolls and gleams with
rivers and lakes. The River Shannon,
Ireland's longest watercourse, drains
the interior reaches. Ancient Gaelic
tribespeople, known as Celts, divided
the land into many kingdoms. Today
four of the ancient provinces, Ulster,
Connaught, Leinster, and Munster,
still outline historic Ireland.*

island lies farther than 60 miles from the sea. To the west the Atlantic binds
the isle; to the east the Irish Sea separates Ireland from Great Britain. The sea
at times has become a protective moat; perhaps its most notable duty was
the sparing of Ireland from invasion by the Romans. Because of its geographic insulation, Ireland became a sanctuary for native traditions. Its in-
sularity affected even the fabled Celts. These aristocratic warriors and
craftsmen who forged a distinctive civilization in northern Europe ended up
absorbing, not displacing, many of the customs and beliefs they encoun-
tered when they reached Ireland sometime in the first millennium B.C.

Because of the Celts, people with Irish surnames—O'Flaherty,
Ryan, McMahon, O'Toole, McCarthy, Kennedy, O'Brien—occasionally
boast that they are descended from kings. Some are. During the period of
the Celtic (or Gaelic) social order—which lingered into the 1600s—Ireland,
at times, was divided into many kingdoms. Each one was centered on a clan
that usually appropriated for its seat of power and faith a venerated hill on
which earlier cultures had left their mysterious stone circles and tombs.

According to legend, a single High King briefly ruled Ireland from
the Hill of Tara. Solemn rooks cawed from a churchyard and sheep scattered as I walked up sacred Tara, a gentle rise in the countryside 20 miles
northwest of the modern seat of government in Dublin. On the well-grazed
summit two earthen mounds ringed by ditches scarcely recall the grandeur

of the hill fort that once stood on this site. Here kings and chieftains met in great assemblies to settle disputes, honor the dead, and indulge in feast and sport. One look at the commanding view, however, and the power of the place becomes clear. A luscious panorama of field and pasture—the central plain of Ireland—opens up at one's feet and spreads to all horizons, green and gold squares like a king's checkered cape flung round his feet. The view from Tara remains an ennobling sight on this island where wealth and prestige still derive so much from the land.

From the summit's edge, the sight of a narrow hollow some 250 yards long stirs one's imagination. A plaque reads "Banquet Hall." Immediately the scene comes to life: a thatched longhouse ringing with boisterous tales of Celtic warriors clad in tunics, smoke rising from enormous roasted boars, wine and mead flowing from flagons, a druid—a pagan priest— whispering omens to the king, and a bard holding court with songs of satire and royal deeds. Alas, only sheep feast in the great hall now.

Besides composing praise poems to the king, the Celtic bard served as a curator of the past, responsible for knowing everything about the reigning clan's lineage. It was this impulse to have light shed on one's ancestors that first drew me to Ireland. I knew from books that my surname O'Neill referred back to a Celtic dynasty—Uí Néill. This lineage ruled Ulster in the north of Ireland off and on for more than a thousand years. One of the dynasty's early ancestors was a Tara king named Niall. It is he who is credited with kidnapping St. Patrick from Britain and bringing him to Ireland as a slave in A.D. 405. But my sights were set on matters more immediate: I wished to see for myself where John O'Neill, my father's father, had been born and to discover if any of his kin still lived in the region.

All that my family knew of the Irish past of John O'Neill (he died when my father was a boy) came from a painting he had left behind. It pictured a valley dotted with ruins, supposedly his Irish home. I longed to visit the place, so one autumn I traveled to it; the area was called Glendalough, Irish for "valley of the two lakes." I found it a restful hollow fringed with heather in the Wicklow Mountains south of Dublin. Penned between the high shoulders of pine-clad slopes stood the remains of a medieval monastic community. The monastery had thrived during the golden age of Irish Christianity, from the sixth to the ninth centuries. During this period Irish monks and holy men established centers of faith and learning renowned throughout Europe. The monks introduced a written language—Latin—to Ireland. With their writing and drawing skills, they transcribed the Bible into magnificent illuminated manuscripts. Behind the ruins, which included a roofless 12th-century church and a 100-foot-high stone tower, two small lakes glimmered. They were just as my grandfather's painting had shown.

I checked into a bed-and-breakfast inn, and before long everyone in the area seemed to know that an American had arrived looking for his roots. No one was shy about coming up to me and trying to puzzle out the whereabouts of any O'Neills. But after two days of looking and questioning I had no leads. Disappointment began to hound me.

On the night before I was to leave—a moonless, windy night, when deer in their rut were screaming on the hillsides—a young woman came to my door. She didn't give her name, but she said that my search had ended. She knew an O'Neill who had the right blood.

Encouraged, I headed out early the next morning. I drove to a whitewashed farmhouse on a hill outside the village of Rathdrum, about ten miles from Glendalough, and knocked on the door. Through a glass pane I could see a flushed woman, perhaps in her 50s, peeking around the kitchen door. "What do you want?" she said suspiciously.

"I'm from America, and I think I'm related to you," I blurted out. Hearing this, the woman ran to the door and flung it open. She threw her arms around me and cried out in a girlish voice, "I've been praying for this all my life." Bridie O'Neill led me inside. For the next several hours we pored over old family photographs, giddily comparing my eyes and jawline with those of her relatives. A family tree indicated that Bridie's grandfather was a brother to my great-grandfather, who she guessed was a cobbler named Tom. "Your grandfather John went to America like so many of us," Bridie said with a touch of sadness. "The O'Neills never wrote back, and so we never knew what happened to all of them."

The following day, Bridie showed me a stone farmhouse in the next valley north of Glendalough. It was in this place, she said, that my great-great-grandfather Patrick had sired 22 children. In the tumbledown graveyard beside the ruins of the monastery we found his stone. The names and dates lettered on it had become faint through the years, and we passed our hands over it as if the stone had been scripted in sacred Braille.

Since my emotional introduction to Ireland that autumn a decade ago, I have returned several times, and always in late summer or early fall when the countryside appears to shed an outer skin. The Irish bogs, those great waterlogged peatlands, turn the color of marmalade; hayfields mellow from green to gold following the harvest; treeless mountains darken with the deep purple of heather.

The close of summer marks the time of many rural fairs and festivals where, as playwright John M. Synge observed, "a crowd is as exciting as champagne" to people in from the farms. Particularly social is the Matchmaking Festival at Lisdoonvarna. Normally a quiet resort at the edge of the Burren, Lisdoonvarna rings with gaiety every September. Like a cloud of blackbirds, farm people from miles around light on the town for holiday after the harvest. The autumn jamboree also marks the time when single people from the countryside come in search of the right mate.

"Every farmer from Tipperary and Limerick must be here," exclaimed Margaret O'Dea, a talkative, stylishly dressed woman whose face was aflame from dancing. At 11 a.m. the ballroom across from the sulfur springs was already jammed with aging couples dancing hand in hand. One, two, three; one, two, three; they swept along to the polka-like music. Partners seemed to change with every number. The expressions on many of the women appeared stony, as if dancing were an unaccustomed activity. Many of the men's faces were lit with excitement, however, as if their bodies were thawing in a hurry after lonely months of work on the farm.

"I met my husband here over 25 years ago," Margaret said. "I'm just here from Dublin today for the 'crack'—to have fun. But you know, a lot of bachelors have no other way to meet a woman than to come here. I sure could show them some rich widows," she said, scanning the crowded room. "I'll warn the men though that women here are getting more Americanized; they don't want to marry a fellow just to look after him."

Before the day was done, I had waltzed with a nun, had my fortune read by a toothless gnome with a pack of soiled playing cards, and had been teased by a trio of women from County Donegal who demanded that I leave the premises because of the wedding ring on my finger.

For sobering up and cooling down, no better spot exists than the Cliffs of Moher, a short drive away. The ocean wind slapped my face, while 650 feet straight down waves clawed at the foot of the palisades. One of the most dramatic sights in Ireland, the five-mile-long Cliffs of Moher rear out of the water like the walls of an impregnable fortress. Noisy seabirds nest on ledges and in cracks. As the sun crosses the sky, the cliffs change colors like a chameleon, shading from green to gray to a fiery gold. Ireland's Atlantic coast is studded with such unforgettable scenery—chiseled headlands, tucked-away coves, half-moon beaches—but rarely does it all come together as forcefully as it does farther south on the Dingle Peninsula.

Marking the westernmost point of habitation on Europe's continental shelf, Dingle is a spur of mountain-tossed land in County Kerry. The peninsula's narrow roads dawdle between tall, flowering hedges until, without warning, they burst onto remarkable views. Among the best are the sandy promenade of Inch Strand, which reaches a vanishing point in the ruffled waters of Dingle Bay, and the gothic profiles of the Blasket Islands, seen from a winding road atop the Slea Head cliffs.

Just as the sights of Dingle captivate, so may the sounds. Traditional Irish music flowers regularly, I'd heard, in the pub of the Dún an Óir Hotel on the peninsula's far end. On the night I stopped by, a flutist from County Kerry, a piper from County Limerick, and a fiddler from New York were engaged in an impromptu session at a corner table. They had begun the night as strangers but had soon discovered their common love of folk music. Spritely jigs and reels were now springing from their instruments. Unlike the Scottish bagpipes, the Irish *uilleann* (elbow) pipes are played by pumping a bellows positioned under the elbow. Later, as the young musicians were starting to flag, a bartender—wearing taps on his shoes—eased onto the floor and began clicking out a fast tattoo. His back stayed rigid and his face was a blank. But his legs were alive, flashing up and out in scissors kicks while his voice whispered "Faster, faster" to the revived musicians.

Down the road in the village of Ballyferriter, I concentrated on the bold rhythms animating Keane's Pub. The arresting sounds were the spoken words of the old Irish tongue. *"Sláinte mhaith,"* the patrons would toast, raising drinks to each other's health. Their language gusted forth, a Celtic dialect full of guttural and sibilant sounds. Irish speech persists mostly in isolated pockets in the west. Such Irish-speaking areas are designated as the Gaeltacht. The language has been dying for more than a hundred years; only 55,000 of the island's 5,000,000 population still use it as the language of the home. Yet judging from what I was hearing at Keane's this particular night, its practitioners are avid keepers of the flame.

"The Irish had their own language before the English even had an alphabet," Breandán Ferriter said proudly. He is director of Radio na Gaeltachta, the national Irish-language network. "English is full of clichés," Mollie O'Connor from Dunquin told me. "Irish is more precise. If you translate an Irish-language novel into English, it ends up as fat and floating as James Joyce's *Ulysses.*"

Mollie may have been exaggerating, but partisan spirits were running high. And so into the night, long past the official closing time of 11 o'clock, the pub crackled with the language of monks and high kings, until a peep of English sounded monotonous, even traitorous.

The Irish language, fair days, legends of St. Patrick and the early Christian monks can quickly stir national passions. In the popular imagination such vestiges of the Celtic past belong to the island's heroic days—that is, to the time before the "strangers" arrived. In the ninth century, Vikings sailed their dragon-bowed longboats up Irish rivers. The invaders sacked monasteries and terrorized farmsteads. The Norsemen also implanted the first towns in Ireland.

French-speaking Normans came next, their regiments of archers and armor-clad knights storming in from western England in the 12th century. Unsupervised vassals of the English crown, the Normans carved out feudal lordships. The new territories sprouted thick-walled castles and hundreds of tower houses whose ruins dramatically color the landscape. From the intermarriage of Normans and the native population came some of the most distinctively Irish surnames, like FitzGerald, Burke, and Joyce.

Naked conquest became the rule by the end of the 16th century. Fearful that Spain or France would exploit Ireland's strategic geographical position and its restless Catholic populace, Queen Elizabeth dispatched English troops to the island. With the routing of the last of the rebel Gaelic chieftains—Hugh O'Neill and Hugh O'Donnell—in 1601 at the Battle of Kinsale, England seized control of Ireland. It was the first of many colonies that would become the British Empire.

The legacy born of English conquest has played a momentous role in shaping Ireland. On the positive side, Ireland inherited her parliamentary traditions and laws from England. English patronage transformed provincial Dublin into a cosmopolitan capital in the 18th century. In addition, the Anglo-Irish, as the Protestant descendants of the British in Ireland were known, produced such outstanding literary figures as Jonathan Swift, W. B. Yeats, and George Bernard Shaw.

In general, however, British rule subjugated the Irish people. Cruel penal laws enacted by the English Parliament outlawed the Catholic Mass and denied Catholics the right to vote, hold public office, and speak Irish. As a result of the repression, the Roman Catholic Church became a powerful symbol of Irish autonomy (the church's pervasive influence continues in Irish society today). English landlords, who ended up owning most of the island, reduced the majority of their Irish tenants to poverty. Emigration to Australia and America in the 19th century practically halved the population.

Only after three centuries of English domination did the force of Irish nationalism prevail. In 1922, the Irish Free State was born. The independent Republic of Ireland comprises 26 of the island's 32 counties.

An island within an island was created when six northern counties in ancient Ulster, their population two-thirds Protestant, refused to join the emerging Irish nation. Keeping the British flag, the defiant counties became Northern Ireland, which together with Great Britain forms the United Kingdom. The origins of separation go back to the early 1600s when King James I transplanted British settlers—many of them Scottish Presbyterians—to the north on land confiscated from the native Irish. Since then the northeast corner of Ireland has been transformed into an enclave of festering religious animosities spilling over to economic and political spheres. To this day the unrest poisons the life of the entire island.

A war between extremists on both sides presently besieges Northern Ireland. Catholics demand more civil rights; Protestants fear being swallowed up in a Catholic Ireland. Since the latest outbreak of violence began in 1969, assassinations and bombings have killed more than 2,400 persons. Naturally, I was a bit nervous about visiting Belfast, the capital of Northern Ireland and the site of much of the sectarian fighting.

When I arrived, I was surprised to find a grande dame of a city center. Extravagant Victorian buildings lined the streets. The imposing structures had been erected as temples of commerce during the Industrial Revolution when Belfast mills turned out most of the world's linen. The city still looks like a hardworking place. Giant cranes swing over the Harland and Wolff shipyard—where the *Titanic* was built—and at the end of each shift at Short Brothers, the aircraft manufacturing plant disgorges an army of men. Downtown the streets are bustling with traffic.

The uninitiated might never sense Belfast's background of violence—that is, until a policeman mentions that it is illegal to leave a car unattended in the heart of the city because of the possible threat of its being a car bomb. The scars of almost two decades of guerrilla warfare are unavoidable in the segregated working-class neighborhoods. Whether in the Protestant ghettos of East Belfast around the shipyards, or in the Catholic redoubts of the Falls Road or Ballymurphy to the west, the scene is one of grim entrenchment. On treeless streets of terrace housing, hateful and defiant graffiti cover curbs and walls; British troops in battle fatigues patrol on foot or in armored cars; metal grates and barbed wire guard pubs and shops; and the Union Jack or the Irish Tricolor flaps blatantly to warn who may enter an area and who may not.

"You shouldn't think all these people are raving sectarians," cautioned Davy Hammond, a Belfast filmmaker and ballad singer who was showing me the embattled areas. "Most of them are more concerned about their homes and families. If you didn't get into politics, you'd find a lot of allegiances between Catholics and Protestants—their ties to church and land, their pub talk about horses and football. . . ." Davy broke off his thought at the sight of an army patrol approaching.

A drive in the country seemed therapeutic after the close atmosphere of Belfast. Spacious lakes and far-off hills and the rolling Irish farmland kept me company through the north. And who could guess that one of Ireland's most splendid stretches of coast lies an hour's drive north of Belfast in County Antrim? From a plateau, mossy glens fall like pleats toward the sea. Sweeping chalk cliffs face Scotland, as near as 13 miles across the North Channel. Just northeast of Bushmills, a whiskey-distillery town, the natural wonder of the Giant's Causeway leads into the sea. A cooled lava spill 60 million years ago left behind this bizarre train of hexagonal slabs and columns. Irish mythology credits the curious sight to a road thrown down by the giant Finn McCool so he could stalk across the Irish Sea to Scotland.

I left Finn McCool's road behind and drove south to Ireland's other capital. Dublin is more benign than Belfast. Fanned out on both sides of the River Liffey—an invasion route of the Vikings—this well-worn city of more than 500,000 people exudes an Old World graciousness. The 18th-century styling of Dublin appears in its dignified avenues and vistas and in architecture obsessed with symmetry. Block after block, Georgian row houses exhibit two-pillar porches and a fanlight over the front door. Crowds throng the shopping streets; city parks resemble Impressionist canvases with their flower beds and languorous strollers; statues of rebels, patriots, literary geniuses, and saints always seem to be looking over one's shoulder.

Of the country's many celebrated figures, the one I longed to meet was Seamus Heaney, Ireland's most famous contemporary poet. In Dublin, we talked over a pub lunch of smoked salmon sandwiches and pints of Guinness stout. A large, warm man with a thatch of white hair and a broad orator's face, Heaney ruminated about the deep effect of the Irish landscape on the human soul. "Did you know that in the Irish language the word for patriotism—*tírghrá*—means love of land?" he asked delightedly. Heaney is especially moved by the bog, the wild marshy prairie that covers nearly one-fifth of the island. The bog serves a practical need; its soggy black sod when cut out and dried provides wood-scarce Ireland with vital fuel known as turf, or peat. The bog supplies emotional warmth as well.

"I have a feeling in the bog of being in an old place, a still place. It's as if I had crossed a boundary," Heaney mused. "The bog was romantic to me as a boy; it was the only place where men, out cutting turf, lit fires and did the cooking. There are no fences in the bog, either. Everywhere else people work on their own patches. And now, when I walk out in the moss, squirting and squelching, that's where I find my perfect solitude."

The poet's praise inspired me to borrow a pair of high rubber boots and squirt and squelch through a bog myself. The chance came in Connemara, the boulder-strewn region of western Galway. In its stony emptiness this region looks as if the Ice Age had only just retreated. The area contains Connemara National Park, a 5,000-acre retreat near the village of Letterfrack. Much of the parkland is wet, tundra-soft. The spongy growth sucked at my heels, and purple moor grass parted stiffly at knee level as I set foot on bog. A musky smell rose from ground saturated from an average of 250 days of rain a year. All around me rivulets of water gurgled unseen beneath the tall grass. A weak October sun glowed, casting the sepia tint of an antique photograph on the still scene. The air was delicious.

My guide, 35-year-old superintendent Noel Kirby, pulled up a clump of lettuce-green sphagnum moss; he wrung it out like a sponge to demonstrate how its cells fill with water. The mushy peat beneath us was about 95 percent water and the rest semi-decayed vegetation. Over millions of years, under the right conditions, these elements could produce coal. Because the bog is acidic, Noel explained, things buried in it tend to be preserved. Turf cutters have come across mummified bodies, gold jewelry from the Celts, even ancient wooden vessels full of butter.

"There's no such thing as virgin wildland in Ireland," Noel said as we tramped along. "In the park we're coming across megalithic tombs, lazy-beds—raised outlines of former crop beds—and prehistoric farm walls." The park was pieced together during the 1970s to save at least some bog acreage from continuous use as pastureland and turf banks. Sheep grazing and turf cutting have eroded sizable portions of the island's bogland. The new park also serves to shelter a small, reintroduced herd of native red deer. The bog doesn't seem to slow the fleet-footed animals. They bound effortlessly through their marshy home.

Noel and I finished the hike by climbing up through bog and heath to the top of 1,460-foot-high Diamond Hill. From its rubbly heights the land to the southwest appeared to sparkle with sequins as sunlight glanced off dozens of small, glacier-scoured lakes. That far vista encompassed Derrygimlagh Bog. John Alcock and his copilot Arthur Brown crash-landed safely there in June 1919, after completing the first nonstop transatlantic flight. To the southeast the bare knuckles of the Twelve Bens, a set of quartzite pinnacles, scraped the sky. Below us from a grassy bowl of the mountains came the faint roar of a waterfall. Up here the world seemed pure and grandiose, high ground fit for a Celtic king, or any climber with poetry in his heart.

So many places in Ireland embody a powerful attraction, I found, that reaching a destination often involves an act of pilgrimage. It may be organized, as when fervent Catholics pour in by bus and plane to the village of Knock in County Mayo, where in 1879 the Virgin Mary was said to have appeared. Or the journey may be a private bow of recognition, as when literary pilgrims travel to the Norman keep of Thoor Ballylee where Yeats wrote poetry, or to the Martello Tower on the Dublin coast where James Joyce briefly lived and where a museum to his work stands.

My special trek brings me back to the purple hills of Wicklow, where I pay homage to my ancestors. Just like the first time, I stop by to talk family with Bridie O'Neill in front of her cottage hearth. Then together we retrace our steps through the brambly graveyard of Glendalough to where the family stone keeps its vigil. Like most pilgrims in Ireland, I too am tapping the strength that lives like a magic eel in the island's deep, mirror well of the past. Bridie and I kneel on the ground of the early monks and tear away a shroud of weeds and briars from the O'Neill stone, exposing the engraved lettering that helps tell our own time-wreathed stories. I can see the marker now; it is shining, like all the living stones of Ireland.

*T*raffic hustles past the colonnaded facades of O'Connell Street in Dublin, the capital of the Irish Republic. Wide avenues, Georgian architecture, and wrought-iron lampposts recall Dublin's prosperity in the 18th century under British rule. Nine centuries earlier, Vikings sailed up the River Liffey and founded the town. Today, graceful crossings, such as the Ha'Penny Bridge (above), span the river. Along its quays have strolled some of Ireland's and the world's finest writers: James Joyce, Samuel Beckett, W. B. Yeats.

*H*orse dealers haggle over ponies (below), while a buyer and seller (opposite) discuss a white-blaze chestnut at the Puck Fair in the town of Killorglin. Customarily, a middleman brings horse traders together, the slapping of hands punctuates the negotiations, and a pat of earth on the horse's hindquarters shows that a bargain has been struck. Horses have excited passions in Ireland ever since the Celts introduced their favorite sport, horse racing. Today, 30 racetracks across the island attract crowds, and unofficial races, "flapper meetings," spring up in the countryside.

FOLLOWING PAGES: *Time slowly vanquishes the thick walls of Dunluce Castle, a 14th-century Norman stronghold that crowns pastoral heights on the Antrim coast of Northern Ireland.*

old visage of Ireland, the Cliffs of Moher plunge from a quiet meadowland in County Clare. The sandstone and   *shale headlands provide ledges for puffins, kittiwakes, and other seabirds. Atop the promontory stands O'Brien's*

Tower, built as a teahouse for 19th-century travelers crossing one of Ireland's most majestic settings.

Off Kinvara, crewmen of the Tonai—a Galway hooker—tidy the jib and ready the mainsail for lowering at the close of the annual Turf Race. As the workhorses of Galway Bay, hookers carried turf, fish, and other supplies to islands and shore towns. Trucks and ferries took over the hauling jobs in the 1960s and left these antique boats to the realm of sport and recreation. On a mural in Kinvara (below) an Irish inscription advertises "The Boat Shop," recalling the era when the village thrived as a boat-building center on Ireland's blustery west coast.

Flaming hair and freckles of a colleen display two unmistakable Irish characteristics. With nearly half its population under 25, Ireland struggles to keep its young people on the island. High unemployment in the republic and in Northern Ireland has spurred more than 140,000 Irish since 1981 to head for the United States, Australia, and other countries. In the 18th century, a quarter of a million people abandoned Ulster in the north to search for opportunity in "Americay." Many Scotch-Irish fought in the American Revolution. Mass emigration has both saved and saddened the lives of the Irish. Rural poverty, deepened by the Great Potato Famine of the 1840s, forced almost half of Ireland's population to leave their home shore between 1845 and 1900—some five million people in all. For many, their last glimpse of Ireland was of the steeple of St. Colman's (opposite) as they sailed from Queenstown, now called Cobh.

FOLLOWING PAGES: Pollnacappul Lough shimmers with reflections of Kylemore Abbey. Built in the 1860s, the manor now serves as a girls' school and a convent for Benedictine nuns.

*Tiny man-made fields lace Inisheer,
smallest of the Aran Islands off western
Ireland. Soil enriched over the years with
seaweed, sand, and manure yields crops*

As a precaution against Atlantic gales on the Aran Island of Inishmaan, rope and pegs secure thatch on a whitewashed farmhouse. Old-style cottages, such as this one, are disappearing from the Aran countryside; islanders now prefer metal-roofed bungalows heated with bottled gas instead of dried turf. Content in its barn stall, a Connemara pony (opposite) shows off its braided mane. This muscular breed, native to the rocky foothills of Connemara in western Ireland, possesses great stamina and agility, especially in jumping.

FOLLOWING PAGES: Church steeples punctuate the resort of Clifden, nestling below the Twelve Bens range in Connemara. Nearby in Derrygimlagh Bog, the first transatlantic flight touched down in 1919, bringing the modern world even closer to this Old World land bound by the sea.

BALI
Realm of Pageantry and Fire

By Cynthia Russ Ramsay.   Photographs by Nicholas DeVore III.

Sunrise flares by Mount Agung on the Indonesian isle of Bali. The 10,308-foot volcano, revered as the abode of the gods, commands this fabled realm of imposing deities and supernatural beings.

At first there was only the distant music, floating through the tree-shaded village in a stream of resonant sound. As it grew louder and rang with the clangor of brass, the long procession came into view—hundreds of people moving quickly down the narrow, dusty road. In the lead were about 20 men in batik sarongs, gravely beating out the sonorous rhythms on gongs, cymbals, and drums.

Not far behind were the women, perhaps 40 of them, all with flowers in their glossy black hair. They were walking with graceful ease as they carried on their heads trays heavy with votive offerings—fruits, flowers, and tinted rice cakes arranged in artistic designs two feet high.

"Why are the people stopping at the crossroads?" I asked Made Yastina, my guide, translator, and friend.

"They will hold a ceremony to welcome deities to the celebration in one of the village temples," he replied. "And since spirits move in a straight line, an intersection is a good place to summon them from all directions."

I was not surprised, for we were in Bali, an island abounding in supernatural beings—which are as much a part of life as rice, motorcycles, tropical flowers, and lofty volcanoes. Appeasing the myriad spirits and gods that populate the Balinese world fills day after day with ritual and pageantry and endows nearly every activity with religious significance—from farming and cockfighting to constructing a house.

In the fading light of sunset, we followed the procession in the village of Kedisan back to a temple with three courtyards. Inside, the glow of oil lamps illuminated that colorful orchestration of piety, cheerful sociability, and drama that characterizes Balinese religious life.

Attendants, all in white, ladled holy water into outstretched palms; men of the food brigade had chopped great mounds of pork, fat, vegetables, and spices for the ceremonial meal; the musicians, seated now, with children beside them or in their laps, filled the air with the shimmering music of a full gamelan orchestra. A woman with flowers in her gray hair stepped forward and with simple sinuous movements and swaying arms danced slowly before the altar. Warrior dancers, brandishing spears and wearing capes and peaked hats, postured fiercely and pranced and whirled with bent knees until the final frenzy of their sham battle. The village girls, taking their turn, moved with more delicate agility, fluttering outstretched fingers and flashing expressive eyes.

This temple festival in a modest mountain village was my introduction to the Balinese religion, which rules the lives of most of the nearly three million people on the island. It is difficult to think of Bali without its deeply felt faith, a blend of animism and Hinduism. This particular mix of beliefs exists nowhere else and sets the island apart from the rest of Indonesia and the world. Though the Balinese venerate Sanghyang Widhi as the Supreme Being of all creation, they direct their daily rituals, worship, and fervor to a galaxy of lesser deities and deified ancestors—who are an anonymous group rather than any specific forebear.

Hindu gods and goddesses of Indian origin coexist comfortably with this pantheon and with a multitude of spirits that reside in rocks, lakes, and in all things of nature. Without their help there is no harvest, no inspiration for the artist, no sale for the merchant. There is also a large population of demons that lurk in the sea, haunt roadways, and menace the night. They cause car wrecks, disease, and mishaps of every sort.

"But even good spirits do bad things, if they are neglected or offended," said Yastina.

To start the day off right, the women of a household make simple offerings in the morning—a few blossoms, some morsels of food, a bit of areca nut. The spirits take only the essence, wafted aloft by burning incense or fanning gestures of the hand. These tokens are everywhere—on the ground for demons, higher up for the deities. Even the shops, market stalls, tourist hotels, and dashboards have these offerings, as do the simple shrines in the fields, under trees, and at sacred places all over the island.

Bali counts tens of thousands of these shrines. Also notable in number are the 10,000-or-more temples, which preside over the landscape with their slender pagoda towers thatched in the black bark fibers of the sugar palm. Each temple celebrates its anniversary, or *odalan*, usually reckoned on a 210-day religious calendar. For the occasion, the gods come down from the mountains and are entertained with music, drama, and dance.

These ceremonies are a community endeavor. Most villages boast at least one gamelan. Some have many more; it's like having a symphony orchestra on every other block. Ketut Rereh is one of the musicians. "I have only 1,600 square meters of *sawah*—irrigated land. It provides rice, nothing more. If I want to buy clothes, I have to do daily labor on roads or construction. My pleasure is to practice and play in the evenings," said Rereh.

A few musicians and dancers are professionals, but most of the performers are bent over their fields by day or sit in classrooms, workshops, or taxis. The beautiful offerings and decorations that crowd the altars are also local productions; women spend many hours cutting, folding, and weaving palm leaves into these works of art.

Bali's incredible ritual life, which calls forth so much time and creative energy, takes priority over business. The owner of a restaurant for tourists told me that she should be able to run her place with at most ten people. "But here I need 30, because there is always some festival going on." For the visitor, on the other hand, the island presents a great verdant stage for a never-ending round of religious spectacles. It seems hard to believe a small island could contain them all.

Only slightly larger than the state of Delaware, Bali is just a speck on the world map. The island lies eight degrees south of the Equator in the sweeping archipelago that constitutes the Republic of Indonesia. Despite its small size, Bali has beguiled countless visitors. Back in the 1930s, when Indonesia was still a Dutch colony, writers, artists, and anthropologists made this South Sea isle famous. They were more impressed by its idyllic villages—where pageantry, art, and beauty are commonplace—than by its miles of beaches and its landscapes of volcanoes, rice terraces, and colorful flowers. Mexican artist-ethnographer Miguel Covarrubias in his widely acclaimed book *Island of Bali* noted: "It was often surprising to discover that an otherwise poor and dilapidated village harboured an elaborate temple, a great orchestra, or a group of actors of repute." For me Bali was a glowing

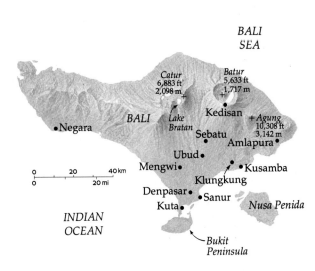

BALI
SEA

INDIAN
OCEAN

Catur
6,883 ft
2,098 m

Batur
5,633 ft
1,717 m

Kedisan

Negara

BALI

Lake
Bratan

Sebatu

Agung
10,308 ft
3,142 m

Amlapura

Ubud

Mengwi

Kusamba

Klungkung

Denpasar

Sanur

Kuta

Nusa Penida

Bukit
Peninsula

0 — 20 — 40 km
0 — 20 mi

Barely larger than Delaware, Bali covers 2,171 square miles, which include volcanic slopes, rain forests, misty lakes, tropical beaches, and hilly scrubland. Balinese delight in staging religious festivals and making elaborate offerings at temples and shrines. They believe that demons haunt the sea, and few venture to fish far from shore. Most of the islanders farm for a living. Their homeland is divine property, they say, and those who work the land lease it from the gods.

experience—each day a carnival of color and music, where even cremations were festive, spectacular events.

"Burning the corpse liberates the soul so that it may attain higher and higher levels of being, until it eventually attains union with the Supreme Being," said Yastina as we set out from the coastal village of Sanur. We were on our way to attend a cremation in the town of Mengwi, about 15 miles to the northwest.

We left the fair-skinned sunbathers to Sanur's tawny beaches and the tourists in outrigger sailing canoes to the area's shallow lagoon. The route led through the capital city of Denpasar, where cars, minibuses, and motorcycles clogged the broad avenues and created bedlam in the lanes.

Once beyond the city, we left the main highway and drove through a realm of rice fields—where plows are still drawn by buffalo and cows—and through villages sheltered from the piercing sunlight by fruit trees and palms. It was midafternoon, and the farmer's workday, which begins with the 4:30 dawn, was over. Men and women were bathing modestly in separate groups in the irrigation canal by the road. Less demure were the laughing, cavorting children. Squatting in little circles were men probably discussing cockfighting. Many of them held trained roosters in their arms, stroking the feathers as they talked; the birds would ultimately shed their blood in combat—either in religious rituals to appease the evil spirits or in illegal gambling matches, where bets are made in a raucous frenzy.

We stopped at a village food stall, where children in school uniforms were waiting their turn. It was a portable snack bar; the food, utensils, and table had all arrived atop the owner's head earlier in the day. Peanuts in tiny bags, bananas, anchovy-size dried fish, rice noodles with sauce served on a banana leaf were standard fare. Steamed sticky rice sweetened with palm sugar seemed to be a favorite. Women run these minirestaurants as well as the village markets; they also raise pigs, chickens, and garden vegetables. It's a separate kitchen economy that gives many of the women income and independence.

As we drove along, the lovely bucolic languor that evokes the Bali of legend was occasionally broken by the roar of a motorbike. The frequent crowing of roosters soon became unobtrusive background noise, but the cacophony of barking dogs roaming in every village did not.

"The curs are supposed to frighten away witches and evil spirits," wrote Covarrubias half a century ago. He concluded that the canines "were undoubtedly provided by the gods to keep Bali from perfection."

Dogs were wandering through the palace compound at Mengwi when I called on Tjokorda Gde Oka. A tall, bold-featured man of great dignity, he behaved like a descendant of one of the powerful princes who had ruled in Bali in times past—which he was.

"We rank the cremation as the most important, most sacred family responsibility," said the Tjokorda, who is almost always referred to by this title—roughly equivalent to His Highness. We were sitting in a building that was half veranda, facing a courtyard where scarlet hibiscus and pink and purple bougainvillea were in bloom and twisting bare branches of frangipani were tipped with crowns of white flowers.

A local palace, or *puri,* has little in common with the imposing structures of Europe or India. Like every residence on Bali, it consists of several low buildings—separate ones for cooking, sleeping, and receiving guests. There is also an area for the family shrines. A surrounding wall encloses the whole compound. No Balinese sleeps comfortably without the wall's protection, for it is a shield from the evil spirits lurking outside. A palace hints at its status with its ornate stone gate and richly carved teak columns and doors painted in red and gold.

Status was even more apparent in the lavish cremation the following day. The corpse, a cousin of the Tjokorda, had been lying in state for five weeks, awaiting the auspicious time for the ceremony. Now a pagoda-like tower—which glittered with tinsel, mirrors, and gilt paper—stood outside the gate, ready to transport the body to the cremation grounds. There the corpse would be cremated in a wooden sarcophagus built to resemble the shape of a bull. Covered in black fabric with golden horns, huge bulging eyes, and a large red tongue, it was at once both gaudy and grand.

In a sudden bustle of activity, the relatives and friends emerged from the palace and carried the shrouded body up the steep, wobbly ramp to a platform near the top of the tower. With crowds shouting encouragement, more than a hundred men knelt and slowly lifted the wide bamboo scaffolding on which the tower rested. It swayed for a moment, and then a boisterous procession, led by musicians, warrior dancers, and members of the family, headed toward the cremation grounds.

Joining the surge was another large group of mourners, also showing little sign of grief. Forty-four families were taking advantage of the occasion to provide their own dead relatives with a grand send-off. The bodies had been temporarily buried years ago, until enough money could be saved to meet the costs of a cremation.

"All this time the souls have been impatiently waiting for release," said Yastina. He explained that bits of bone had been exhumed and would be cremated, along with small sandalwood effigies, on separate mounds near the royal pyre. At the cremation grounds, spectators eddied around the tower and the bull. Vendors had set up their stalls in the shade of trees; tourists bought soda, beer, and bottled water. Balinese slaked their thirst with a sweet drink tinted an intense candy pink.

For a long while the priests chanted prayers and dispensed holy water. Religious events hardly ever take place without water made holy by reciting mystical formulas and by making sacred hand gestures known only to high priests. Relatives of the Tjokorda's cousin crowded round to pay their respects to the deceased. It took about three hours for the fire to consume the bull and the body it contained. As the flames licked higher and higher, the bull's eyes glared eerily in the reddish glow.

"This is only the beginning of the series of rites that will take place over the next months," Yastina said. The funeral agenda includes liberating the soul by cremating its effigy. In the final ceremony the spirit is invited to join the ancestral souls, whose presence in the family is a palpable thing. For example, at a wedding the bride adopts the husband's ancestral gods after she is formally introduced to them. They are informed of births, invited to feasts, and regularly consulted through mediums who are in a trance.

"I will make special offerings to ask my ancestors for their protection on my journey to the United States," said Anak Agung Ayu Mirah. A strikingly beautiful granddaughter of the last feudal ruler of Karangasem, a former regency in eastern Bali, Mirah lives in a rambling palace in Amlapura. I had arrived in the town after taking the only highway east from Sanur. My route led me past Kusamba, where gaily painted outrigger canoes rested on the black sand. The boats ferry cargo and passengers between Bali and Nusa Penida, a small arid island that rests on the southeast horizon like a fallen cloud.

From Kusamba I drove the narrow plain between steep mountains and the sea. It was early afternoon when I reached Amlapura and met Mirah, who led me through the deserted courtyards in the old palace. "I remember when more than 300 people lived here. There was a separate compound for each of my grandfather's wives. He had ten, but never more than seven at one time," she said. On one of the verandas stood a mural-size photograph of a lean, handsome man in a brocade sarong and an embroidered jacket covered with medals.

Like the other princes of Bali, the old radja had staged lavish religious ceremonies with virtually nonstop music and dancing. But Mirah's grandfather, who died at the age of 89, had another extravagance—building palaces. One complex of pools, moats, fountains, statues, and pavilions was constructed at the village of Ujung, another at Tirtagangga, just a few miles away. Part of the palaces' enchantment lies in their tranquil settings. At Ujung we strolled the grounds until darkness dissolved the lovely terraced curves of the countryside, and we watched sacred Mount Agung, where the gods dwell, melt into the starry northern sky.

Though Mirah discourages the use of her title—Anak Agung (Her Highness)—she is proud that her lineage is of the Madjapahit aristocracy. This dynasty, once centered on Java, had ruled a great Hindu empire until the beginning of the 16th century. When Muslim conquerors threatened the Madjapahits, the royal family and its entourage of courtiers, scholars, priests, and artists fled across a narrow strait and took over Bali.

The island may be small, but there was room for nine radjas, who maintained glittering courts and patronized the arts. They also feuded until the Dutch defeated the last independent rulers in the early 1900s. Some radjas negotiated treaties that honored their suzerainty over their people. However, the radja of Badung, who opposed certain Dutch policies, chose to resist. In 1906, outnumbered and dreading the dishonor of exile, he led his followers—men and women—in a fight to the death, a *puputan*.

Seldom has history seen such an army. Wearing their jewels and carrying gem-encrusted daggers, the Balinese set fire to their palaces and left in silent procession. Without wavering, they headed toward the Dutch guns. When they were 70 feet away, they rushed at the invaders in a frenzy. Wave after wave of Balinese fell. The body of their leader lay buried under the corpses of those who had dragged themselves to die next to their king.

Two years later, the last independent rulers—the royal family of Klungkung—also chose a suicidal attack over surrender and a life of disgrace. After the conquest, the Dutch—for the most part—took a passive role. They left local government to the princes, who retained some of their regal trappings and rode around in cars with gold royal insignia on the hood. Even now in Bali, with their fields lost to land reform and their power gone, the princes are highly respected.

Royalty was sustained by the caste system, which separates the nobility—the priests, warriors, and ruling princes—from most of the population. These days common people don't crouch when addressing or passing a member of the high castes, though prominent princes and high priests still receive their bows. Radjas and priests no longer shake their fists at planes overhead, shouting, "How dare they fly people higher than me." Mirah has not been ostracized for marrying outside her caste—to an American. The feudal system *is* on the way out, but for the moment it lingers on.

Caste still affects relationships between people, even determining the languages they speak. For instance, when two men who are strangers meet, they almost immediately ascertain each other's rank in hierarchy by asking, "Where do you sit?" Each response identifies caste. When the man of higher status speaks, he talks down, using Low Balinese—the aboriginal language of the commoners. In return, the man of lower caste shows respect by using the more refined, flowery High Balinese, with its Sanskrit flavor. It's somewhat as if an English earl were to speak in Cockney to a London cabbie, who would reply in a clipped Oxford accent. In Bali, however, such conversations are carried on in two separate and distinct languages. In these more egalitarian times, Bahasa Indonesia—the national language, a Malay tongue—is taught in schools and used in commerce.

I found other customs equally surprising. I told Yastina about a gift I had given to a hostess who took it and put it away, never saying a word.

"Opening the package would have been rude," Yastina explained. "Of course anything you bring would be pleasing. I'm sure your generosity will be returned even though our language doesn't have the words to say 'thank you.' "

Nor are there words to say "good-bye." People simply say *pamit*—"I'm leaving."

For meals, the housewife cooks only once a day, in the morning. People eat when they are hungry. They eat the food cold and often eat it alone, generally viewing the process as a biological function rather than a social occasion.

Otherwise, privacy has little place in the Balinese way of life. Everyone belongs to a variety of groups that bring ties and obligations. The *bandjar*, a neighborhood fraternity in which membership is compulsory for married men, organizes local activities and festivals. Most Balinese know how it works. I heard of one important businessman who chose to forget. For years he neglected his bandjar responsibilities. When his father died, he had to use all his power to persuade the men of the bandjar to carry the funeral tower. They finally did, but not in the direction of the cemetery.

Farmers also belong to a *subak*, a local agricultural society that maintains the irrigation system and organizes the ceremonies that celebrate each stage of rice cultivation. When Yastina and I visited the village of Siangan, due north of Sanur, members of the subak were helping Made Gendra in his rice field. One team pulled seedlings from the nursery plot and set them in bunches on a large tray. Others pushed the green shoots into the muddy ooze, first slapping them in water to clean their roots.

Nearby, fields golden with rice ready for harvest were rigged with a network of strings. Assorted noisemakers to scare birds away dangled from the grid—tin cans with pebbles, bamboo clappers, plastic squares. A woman in a shed on a platform above the field shook the lines to rattle the devices. But the birds were brazen, and her shouts as she jumped down to shoo them away were more effective.

Yastina and I headed down the steep hillside, walking on dikes that enclose each terrace and dam the water when the field is irrigated. We were descending "the stairway of the gods," an apt Balinese description for these spectacular earthworks that sculpture the mountain landscapes. Farmers stagger their planting time, so every field can receive water when it needs it. There is no single harvest season; one vista, therefore, can reveal all the stages of growth: tiny shoots in flooded paddies that glitter like mirrors in the sunlight, rice grown into a vibrant green, tall plants ripened to gold.

Bali's hot, humid climate, seasonal monsoon rains, and fertile soil —constantly enriched by water from streams carrying volcanic ash—produce two to three rice harvests a year on irrigated plots. The fields are never idle. When not growing rice, they yield sweet potatoes, cassavas, soybeans, and peanuts. In the higher elevations, rice gives way to cloves, coffee, and vanilla. The island's bounty of fruits is also lavish: papayas as big as watermelons; dainty sugar-sweet bananas; mangoes; guavas; mangosteens with their succulent white pulp inside a thick magenta rind. And there is durian, smelly but with a custard taste that many people find delicious. Naturalist Alfred Russel Wallace described the white fruit in its brown shell covered with small spikes as "worth a voyage to the East to experience."

Seventy percent of the island's population make their living farming. But a stroll down the streets of Ubud lined with shops and galleries, small restaurants, hotels, and homestays (rooming houses) indicates that people of this village earn their income another way.

"If tourists are interested in culture, they come to Ubud," said Agung Rai. The son of a sharecropper, he started selling paintings to foreigners at 16, hawking at beach hotels in Kuta, about 20 miles away. Now, 15 years later, tourist buses stop outside his art gallery, and painters working cross-legged on the veranda feel fortunate when Rai exhibits their work.

The range of Balinese painting showed itself in the gallery's seven buildings. Many paintings portray scenes of daily life, the canvases crowded with people and vegetation. "Not every visitor wants art. Some just want a memory," Rai told me. "But dealing in art is not like dealing in peanuts. I don't only show what I know most tourists will buy. I look at some of these paintings with my heart, not my eyes."

Painting is also a successful business for the artist I Dewa Nyoman Batuan. He has been at the forefront in developing a style that uses birds and flowers in a vibrant, decorative way. Batuan readily admits, "The floral paintings are like skin—not deep. They have no inside. My secret is that I also make paintings for myself—paintings that show our spiritual values and our faith."

In a similar way, Bali's dancers and musicians profit from the presence of many thousands of tourists but still hold fast to their religious traditions. Those who perform in hotels also return to their villages to honor and entertain their gods. Even in Kuta, a seaside resort blighted with bars and stalls selling T-shirts, every establishment still makes its food and flower offerings to spirits. Around the corner from the discos, religious celebrations still take place on schedule.

"With money coming in from tourism, we now build better temples, have more orchestras, hold bigger ceremonies. More of our young people are learning to play music and to dance," Batuan said.

Since the time of Covarrubias, doomsayers have feared the culture of Bali would "disappear under the merciless onslaught of modern commercialism and standardization." In the old days, the Balinese believed that priests had put an invisible barrier around the island to keep it pure. In fact, for centuries Bali has preserved its culture, while other islands all around succumbed to Islam. Strong ocean currents and treacherous reefs have helped to isolate the island.

Perhaps even greater protection against foreign influences came from the desire to live as their fathers lived—in a close-knit community— close to the gods. Today that commitment to their faith and their way of life is like a wall, which so far has shielded the Balinese culture from many destructive effects of tourism.

Will Bali remain a world apart and retain its magical union of life, religion, and art? Weeks of exploring the island had brought me to this question. I sat down in a pavilion on Ubud's main street and stared across a lotus pond toward an old temple. From somewhere—as if to answer me—came music like the tinkle of soft sweet bells wafting through the air.

A genius for music, a gift for dancing endow life in Bali with a special charm and grace. Celebrated dancer Imade Djimat (right) demonstrates stylized movements of the fingers to his class. Wearing tiaras of gold leaf and fragrant flowers, dancers (top) gather for photographs. For the most part, only local amateur talent performs at temple ceremonies, weddings, and the religious events that bring pageantry to the smallest villages. The musicians above wear white, the traditional color for religious ceremonies. Drums, gongs, cymbals, and the metallaphone with bronze keys (above) produce the gamelan orchestra's shimmering sounds.

*In a sacred morality play, a flat leather
puppet performs as a moving shadow on
a lighted cloth screen. A single versatile
puppeteer, called a* dalang, *manipulates
a large cast of these silhouette characters,
controlling them by thin sticks attached
to the bodies. Sitting cross-legged behind
the screen, beneath a flaring oil lamp,
the dalang begins the show by chanting
magic formulas to protect the puppets.
He also invokes the divinity patronizing
the performance. In a virtuoso one-man
show that may last from late evening
until dawn, the dalang plays every role,
changing the exaggerated tones of his
powerful voice depending on the
character portrayed. Movements of the
puppets' arms, jointed at the shoulder
and elbow, emphasize the dialogue.
Tinkling background music heightens
the eerie dramatic effect of the phantom
figures in the flickering light. The divine
and royal characters chant or speak in
the ancient Kawi language; the bawdy,
witty clowns, who delight the audience
with jokes and slapstick, speak Low
Balinese. Although few islanders
understand Kawi, they easily follow the
action because they know the tales, most
derived from Hindu epics. Staged at
many celebrations of the Balinese faith,
the* wayang kulit, *or shadow play,
portrays the endless struggle between
good and evil.*

*B*alancing offerings for the gods, two women pay a visit to a temple. On holidays, when deities visit mortals, the islanders entertain their divine guests with food, music, and dance. Banners decorate temple grounds (opposite) near the village of Sebatu. Spring water pours into sacred pools where people cleanse themselves for temple ceremonies.

FOLLOWING PAGES: Farmers harvest rice on hillsides stairstepped with terraces.

*I*n central Bali, a rice field owes its bumper crop to sound farming practices, an elaborate irrigation system, and numerous religious rituals. Farmers often pay tribute to Dewi Sri, the rice goddess, with a bouquet offering (below, left). When grain first appears on the stalk, Balinese say the "rice is pregnant" and make offerings of eggs and sour fruits. Harvest rites may include a cockfight to appease evil spirits with spilt blood. A rooster in a bamboo case (below, right) arrives at a village building crowded with caged fighting cocks.

*R*outine drill: Herded ducks march into paddies to eat worms, snails, and rice grains spilled during harvest.

Wherever the herder plants the bamboo rod, the ducks will stop and forage. The flock never strays far from the marker,

even if the herder leaves. At day's end,
when the farmer holds the pole high, the
ducks line up and waddle home.

$\mathcal{W}$ind-driven mist from the Indian Ocean and a booming surf assault a beach in western Bali. Few roads penetrate the untamed interior of this region. In the bush country of the western uplands, deer and wild hogs roam. Far to the south, in certain coves facing the Bukit Peninsula, breaking waves spray the ruined foundations of ancient sea temples. In this area, Bali's

*southwestern coast begins its sweeping
curve westward toward Java. Sparsely
settled, western Bali unrolls miles of
bewitching seascapes treasured by
seekers of solitude.*

At a ritual cremation, flames leap toward a tiger-shaped sarcophagus (opposite) containing the remains of a priest. The fire frees the soul for its next incarnation, the Balinese believe. Though saddened, they regard a funeral as a time for rejoicing. Below: Men carry a sarcophagus; bearers will bring the corpse later, atop an ornate tower. At the cremation grounds, a high priest recites prayers and presides over the lighting of the fire. Days of elaborate ceremonies precede and follow this grand and expensive send-off for the soul.

FOLLOWING PAGES: Temple tiers, like these of Ulun Danu, rank Balinese gods, 11 denoting the highest. Ulun Danu salutes the water goddess Dewi Danu, one of Bali's most revered deities.

NEW ZEALAND
From Snowy Peaks to Sparkling Rivers

By Tom Melham.   Photographs by Paul Chesley.

"Cloud in the Sky," Mount Cook lives
up to the name Polynesian settlers gave
it. The summit, at left above, crowns
Mount Cook National Park as well as
the Southern Alps of New Zealand.

The sun had set—but Mount Cook refused to sleep. Although all its jagged, snow-clad neighbors had blushed rose and varied their color through deepening reds into pale violets and finally gray, Cook remained incandescent, its icy faces seeming to glow from somewhere within rather than from mere shreds of a departed sun. Even the arrival of stars and a crescent moon did not persuade this giant to submit to night; it continued to stand out from the surrounding palisades like a pale beacon in the wilderness. At 12,349 feet it is New Zealand's highest mountain, more than 800 feet higher than its tallest rival. Thus it clings to the sun's colors longer than other peaks, longer often than the clouds. Several thousand feet below Cook's distinctive, rooflike summit, a thin streamer of fluff had impaled itself, recalling the mountain's ancient Maori name: *Aorangi,* or "Cloud in the Sky," bestowed more than 11 centuries ago by those seafaring Polynesians who first settled New Zealand. Even today, the name fits.

An hour later, Aorangi was invisible. Night had not triumphed—clouds had, suddenly packing together in a dense overcast not 300 feet above the mountain's base. Such whiteouts are common in this alpine island nation, whose western flank zooms up from zero elevation to more than 10,000 feet in as little as 22 miles. The sharp ascent thrusts warm, wet ocean air to chilly heights where the moisture must condense. Often the resulting clouds stack up in unending ranks along the Main Divide, ultimately rolling over it like ocean breakers coming ashore. And like the surf, these frontal attacks can be entrancing, almost magical to behold.

Mountains are but one of innumerable natural splendors to grace New Zealand, a Colorado-size country stretched across 13 degrees of latitude—about the same span as the western coast of the contiguous United States. It possesses extraordinary diversity and compactness, its seagirt borders enclosing rain-forested wildernesses, fjords as dramatic as Norway's, smoking volcanoes and spewing geysers, finger lakes full of trout, tussocky hills full of game, native plants and animals that exist nowhere else, crashing white-water streams, jagged seaside cliffs, pancake rock formations, inland caves, and dramatic undersea arches and reefs. Acre for acre, New Zealand has more scenic and topographic variety than any other country—all of which makes it an outdoorsman's dream come true.

Nature has split this land into two major isles, the North Island and the South Island. The more temperate and less rugged North claims volcanoes past and present, rolling hills, and countless beaches and bays. Smaller in size than its southern counterpart, it nevertheless harbors two-thirds of the nation's 3.3 million people and most of its industry; yet it prides itself as much on its seashores as it does on its commerce. The country's major metropolis—Auckland—calls itself The City of Sails, tipping its hat to the colorful pleasure craft that dot its waters like confetti whenever the sun shines. In the 1920s, American author and outdoorsman Zane Grey dubbed a stretch of this island's northeastern coast "the angler's El Dorado" after plumbing its abundant supply of marlin, tuna, and other game fish. His label is even more apt today, for the area draws spearfishing scuba divers, as well as anglers in all types of boats from sail to jet. Jet boating, by the way, is a New Zealand invention to cope with shallow local streams and rivers.

In contrast, the South Island boasts Mount Cook and the neighboring confusion of snowcapped peaks and ridges known as the Southern Alps. Though continental giants such as Alaska's McKinley or Africa's Kilimanjaro tower far higher, this island's corrugated backbone is astonishingly compact and challenging. The South Island's features include, for example, steep-walled fjords and hanging valleys born of glaciers, brown sand beaches and dazzling icefalls, crystalline lakes and rivers, hardwood forests and broad plains. The magic of New Zealand is that all these varied features—and the different climates they create—coexist so close together. No place in the country lies more than 80 miles from the sea, and none escapes the sea's influence. So it is that one can ski an inland mountain, then windsurf off the coast—all in the same day.

Though the bedrock here is ancient, today's convoluted topography is not. "Basically, what you see is all very young," says Dr. Richard I. Walcott, a geology professor at Victoria University of Wellington. He adds that the mountains outside Wellington, the nation's capital, "have arisen out of the sea only within the last million years, probably the last half million—an *instant* of geologic time."

For almost all its existence, New Zealand remained rather flat and low-lying. It originated from massive river deltas that built up off Australia and Antarctica hundreds of millions of years ago, when the two continents were united. As recently as 80 million years ago the huge tectonic plates that underlie earth's crust moved in such a way that these deltas began to split off from their mother continents; rifts spawned the Antarctic Ocean and the Tasman Sea. New Zealand eventually wound up atop a no-man's-land where two plates, the Pacific and the Indo-Australian, happened to meet.

To the north, the Pacific plate dives under the Indo-Australian. To the south, the Indo-Australian crunches under the Pacific. In between, especially beneath the South Island, the plates clash head on, resulting in surface crumpling that produced the Southern Alps. These mountains, according to Walcott, "started rising about five million years ago, maybe only two million. The whole area now is coming up very fast—about 10 millimeters a year, perhaps as much as 20 millimeters in some places"—about half an inch to an inch. At that rate, the Alps would balloon six to twelve *miles* in elevation every million years.

Why aren't they that tall today? For one thing, the uplift hasn't been constant. For another, the mountains have created an intriguing equilibrium: They erode precisely as fast as they rise. The nearby ocean provides unlimited moisture, prompting high precipitation along the Alps—the equivalent of more than 30 feet of rain a year, says Walcott.

"That's what is causing the erosion," he adds. "And there's not much doubt what's causing this high rainfall—it's the mountains. So we have a feedback mechanism; as mountains push higher, they cause more precipitation, which increases erosion, eventually balancing the uplift."

Most of that precipitation takes the form of snow on the Southern Alps. Billions of gentle crystals descend yearly, accumulating in such masses that their combined weight eventually compresses earlier snowfalls into ice. Glaciers result—slow, grinding rivers of ice powered by gravity. As they descend the slopes, their ice stretches and compacts, giving rise to avalanches, icefalls, crevasses, and rockslides. Mindful of such hazards, New Zealanders respect glaciers. They also ski down them.

Skiing is a popular activity in this mountainous land, whose Southern Hemisphere location makes it the ideal training camp for world-class skiers during the Northern Hemisphere's summer. All classes of skiers enjoy New Zealand's glacier skiing and "heli-skiing"—the chartering of helicopters to haul skiers up rugged mountains.

The Tasman Glacier lies just east of Mount Cook, hemmed in by the South Island's Main Divide and another jagged ridge. Single-engine skiplanes ferry you and your guide—today it's Don McFadzien—to a spot called Tasman Saddle. From here the Tasman sprawls 18 miles downhill, dropping more than a vertical mile in the process. At your feet lie some 20 square miles of totally untrampled snow, fresh from the night before. The day dawns cloudless, every jag and pinnacle leaping at you, sharply etched against the blue, blue sky. The air is so transparent, the sun so sparkling, that the eye grossly foreshortens distances. From the glacier's summit, Mount Cook appears to be only a mile or two away—but it's actually *twelve*, from peak to peak.

You and Don push off, reveling in what must be man's closest approximation to flight without actually leaving the ground. No prepared trails mark the way; you chart your own course through nature's raw puffery, soaring right or left, up or down, wind song filling your ears. Like a vast cloud bank, the glacier's surface lies fractured into a fantasy land of freeform shapes, all marshmallow and meringue. Huge tidal waves hang over you frozen in time; shark's teeth jut from a rumpled palisade; craters alternate with dunelike billowings. Against this sculptured whiteness, an ice cave's blue gash stands out like a patch of sky against solid overcast. You drop down inside, momentarily trading sun's harsh glare for the soft, sheltering blue glow within, then cruise out the far end—and skim over a windblown plateau ashimmer with ripply textures of watered silk.

The immediacy of Don's voice yanks you from the Tasman's dreamlike spell: "In about a half hour, things will start falling off around here."

Only minutes later, the warming sun verifies his prophecy: a distant, explosive crackling signals the collapse of a minor icefall above. It also reminds you that the very glacier under your skis is not solid but a Swiss cheese of ever changing pits and crevasses, camouflaged over with snow bridges. These gaps can be treacherous—or a godsend.

"They're good places to hide," Don explains, recalling a sudden storm that turned a day hike into an overnight bivouac. Without a tent, he and his companions camped in a crevasse. It was no accident that Don found a safe place; he has favorite crevasses that he seeks out. "Where the snow flows away from the mountain, there's a bit of a slot in there, and you just drop inside. OK—it's not five-star hotel stuff, but you're out of the wind and the spindrift. You're much safer in a little hole like that than wandering around in a blizzard, where you're losing energy so fast," he says.

It's hard to exaggerate the importance of life-style to residents of New Zealand. Young or old, they tend to love the land and the outdoors, to

Twin landmasses, the North Island and
South Island—along with hundreds of
outlying isles—constitute New
Zealand. Beaches, bays, and fjords
sculpt the coasts, and forests, rivers, and
lakes distinguish inland areas.
Polynesians, ancestors of the Maori,
arrived here more than a millennium
ago. In 1769, famed British explorer
James Cook mapped 2,400 miles of New
Zealand's coastline; Mount Cook and the
strait linking the two main islands bear
his name. Today, the North Island
contains most of the country's 3.3
million residents, and the South Island
boasts most of the country's rugged
wilderness. In Mount Cook National
Park alone, 140 peaks of the Southern
Alps soar more than a mile high. The
nation offers an array of indigenous and
imported life-forms. From one species of
flightless bird, found only here, New
Zealanders took their nickname "Kiwi."

revel in the daily adventures and challenges they can find there, preferring
to live what they perceive as a full life rather than to focus solely on salary.
Many careers are not confined to the indoors, nor is wilderness merely a
stage for sport. To many residents, such as Don, the land and its various
challenges create an alluring way of life.

Don has spent the past five of his 33 years guiding skiers down the
Tasman and climbers up Mount Cook and other peaks. He's seen local
winds jump from zero to 40 knots in less than an hour and has weathered
storms that "can dump two meters of snow just like that."

Over time, the volatile weather and the enormous popularity of the
country's rugged scapes among hikers, climbers, and skiers have moved

the nation to evolve a hut system that ranks among the world's best. Cabins—usually stocked with bunks, mattresses, stoves, and other supplies—are found in many national parks, national forests, and other reserves, as well as on some private lands. They exist not just in the hazardous high country, but also in frequently hiked areas such as the Milford Track, where they help reduce human wear on the wilderness.

In fact, New Zealand boasts so many huts and trails that Brin Barron of the New Zealand Forest Service maintains: "It's becoming more difficult, nowadays, to get into danger in the bush."

The "bush"—a term embracing native forests as well as scrub—is where Brin puts in most of his work time, as a professional hunter. His quarry is not elk or other game but feral goats, descendants of those introduced more than two centuries ago by settlers and prospectors. Today, the forest service considers goats harmful to native vegetation and responsible for aggravating erosion, so much so that it employs Brin and other hunters to control the animals' numbers.

I spent several days with Brin patrolling the tussock and grassland near the Shotover River in central South Island, where icy streams and steep ravines alternate with sharp ridges. The land is visually open yet physically tortuous; though you can see for miles, it might take half a day to reach the next ridge just two thousand yards away.

We had set out in a four-wheel-drive Landcruiser, fording the river and bouncing up foothills to a trailhead where we parked and continued on foot. Much of the rock along the Shotover is mica schist—a greasy, flaky laminate of former muds and silts that, like sheets of plywood, come unglued. Find an exposed edge, and you can slide part of one stony layer free without disturbing the others—just as a magician might draw a card from the middle of a deck.

Uplift has broken the schist into sawtooth ridges and offset its layers, imparting a fish-scale texture to the hills, for the underlying rock tends to break and slide off at the slightest touch. Slumps scar the steeper faces; piles of loose scree are common. "It's unstable country, shifting all the time," warned Brin, pointing out collapsed slopes and a gravel flat that only a few years earlier had obliterated a 40-foot-deep lake.

Another challenge here is the vegetation; it includes spear grass, a fearfully sharp, branched version of Spanish bayonet, and matagouri, a woody shrub armed with two-inch-long thorns. Then there's the tussock that overlies the rock like a tufted coverlet: not bad on a level walk, but treacherous on a slope. Its tawny manes can be slippery. Plant a foot anywhere but dead center atop a tussock, and the spongy mass can twist or swivel, thrusting you off-balance and making for a long, tiring day.

Again and again, Brin scrambled up tussocky slopes to the high scrub preferred by goats for its forage and cover. He often dropped his prey with a single shot, ending the day with a tally of 15 goats.

Homeward bound in the Landcruiser, we again had to ford the Shotover—here a fast, hundred-foot-wide channel gouging a far wider gravel wash. As our wheels rammed and slid over the rounded, moving stones, I watched the water climb to within a foot of the window bottom— higher than it had been during our morning crossing. Waves sloshed over the hood. Still, the engine continued to purr. Brin slowed for a tricky stretch of gravel—and suddenly, not quite halfway across the river, we were stuck.

It was not a good spot to be in: crosswise to the current, hung up on a gravel bar, our clutch wet and slipping while the wheels spun uselessly. Brin asked me to get out and push. I opened my door, and a torrent filled the bottom of the cab. Standing waist-deep in the freezing river, we both tried to jerk the Landcruiser off the bar, without success. I had been told that a single heavy rain or sudden thaw could raise the Shotover by 30 feet, over-night. We couldn't just leave things where they were.

Fortunately, a nearby sheep farmer had spotted us and was already on the way in *his* four-wheel-drive. Soon Arthur Borrell—bespectacled, white-haired, and barefoot—jumped out on the sharp gravels of the river bank. He had a snarl of steel cable in tow. Forty minutes later, after a few false starts and a great revving of engines and grinding of gears, we inched free of the river's clutches and rolled ashore. Arthur buzzed off so fast I didn't have the chance to thank him, but Brin assured me not to worry.

"Arthur's hauled people out of the river heaps of times. Been stuck there himself—he knows what it's like."

We headed home for a fire and a cup of Brin's wilderness cure-all: hot tea. Off came soggy shoes; half a pound of gravel spilled from each sock. Later I browsed through the visitor's log common to many New Zealand cabins. This one was filled with ten years' worth of passing comments, an informal history that included an appropriate entry dated May 9, 1985:

"Very deep crossing at 16 mile. Land-Rovers do float."

Memories streamed back of the day's repeated fordings, the endless tramping on cold and wet feet, the noxious matagouri and spear grass that bloodied legs and ripped shirts, the rotten rock—all braved for some un-wanted goats. Who saw the effort, or even the results, I wondered aloud. It seemed the ultimate thankless job.

But to Brin, it's perfect.

"Even if I wasn't hunting—even if I had to cut track or something else—I'd stay on. It's the life-style. You don't have to catch a bus in the morning. Nobody's telling you, 'Do this tomorrow.' You're out there by yourself. If you make any balls-ups, you suffer the consequences. You've got your own freedom. It's a better look at life."

Shotover resident Stuart Ross certainly agrees. At age 71, he's still something of a drifter, leaving his wife and comfortable house in Dunedin for a six months' stay on the Shotover once a year. He holes up in a sparsely furnished hut some ten feet square that lacks plumbing, central heating, or telephone. He leaves his door wide open even on raw days, partly as invita-tion to passersby to stop in and "yarn," partly so he can gaze beyond at the foggy, tussocky, ravined mountains without leaving the fireplace. Stuart has been coming to this hardscrabble country for the past 52 years. Just that is quite an endorsement, for Stuart abhors routine. He maintains with pride:

"You name it, I've done it. I've never stuck to any job longer than five years. If you've been five, you're not interested any more. What's after that? Learn something new."

Stuart Ross might be an engineer by training and a jack-of-all-trades by vocation, but he's a prospector by sheer desire. He handed me a sample of a local pleasure: a two-inch-long nugget of raw gold. Abraded and pitted by the Shotover's constant motion, it gleamed like the trove from King Tut's tomb. It was one of many plucked from these hills and rivers over the years.

Stuart first came to the Shotover long after its 19th-century heyday, when it was known as the world's richest gold-bearing stream. Along the way he managed to pick up a fair bit of geology and mining knowledge. Eventually he developed his own theories on locating gold and began finding it in places where other prospectors had failed or had said it didn't exist. He doesn't get much; not even an ounce a month.

"But I couldn't care less about the money," Stuart proclaims. "No, it's the mental satisfaction. If I get a bit of gold, then my interpretation was right. It's the thinking, the figuring out just where and how nature hides her tiny crumbs of gold amid all that dross. It's not just going down to the river with a dish.

"Boy, I've had my time. I'm out in the fresh air, out in the environment I like. Look, life's what you make it. I've known loads of blokes who wished they'd done this and wished they'd done that. Hell, I've just done it. If there's no bloody pleasure to life, it's not bloody worth living."

The gutsiness and spirited independence behind such words can be found again and again throughout this nation, throughout its past. New Zealand's first settlers—that branch of eastern Polynesians who were the ancestors of today's Maori—obviously were independent and daring, for they sailed open canoes thousands of miles across uncharted seas just to get here, as early as A.D. 800. They discovered a land strange to them, one that lacked the tropical flora and fauna they had known to the north. It had no indigenous mammals except for a few species of bats, and the climate was too cool for the Maori staple—a sweet potato called *kumara*—to overwinter naturally. But the immigrants quickly adapted.

They hunted their new land's richly varied bird life and fished its abundant waters. And they fashioned wood from its vast forests into buildings that included kumara storehouses, thus giving rise to farming settlements. They also developed their own art—carvings, weavings, and tattoos—often embellished with spirals and interlocking images that make up a distinctive, flowing, and dramatic style. Though aspects of their culture were suppressed by the *pakeha*—the whites—the Maori today are reasserting their heritage and are calling the world's attention to their treasured art and traditions.

Whether of pakeha or Maori stock, today's New Zealanders proudly take the nickname "Kiwi" after the pudgy, flightless, and rarely seen native bird that lives only here. The culture of the island nation, however, is largely imported, and the country remains an intriguing blend of the indigenous and the introduced. In the last century, long after the earliest Maori arrivals, English, Scots, Irish, and other Europeans began moving to New Zealand, sparked by dreams of land ownership and driven by raw determination. Where these people found an alien wilderness they carved out their own ideas of perfection. They stripped away much of the native forest and scrub, replacing the tree ferns, spiky "cabbage trees," and unfamiliar conifers with grassy paddocks subdivided by windbreaks of willow and Lombardy poplar that mimicked farms they had left behind. They and their descendants sought to import the best that the Western world had to offer. Visit any New Zealand town in springtime, and even the plainest house on the block often boasts an extravagance of azaleas and other introduced flowers of bright colors. Cities such as Wellington and Christchurch today harbor vast botanical gardens that feature everything from formally clipped roses to stands of native rain forest.

Other imports that have flourished in this land are the rainbow and brown trout that flash through clear inland waters. European red deer and North American elk join chamois, thar, and other game animals introduced to New Zealand's forests. All took advantage of the country's lack of large predators and its abundance of fodder. Red deer reached such numbers that they were classed as vermin and were hunted for their skins and meat. Today, they are no longer pest but resource; deer farmers seek wild deer for breeding purposes in hopes of expanding the world venison market. Thus does import become export. The same is true of many "New Zealand" fruits—apples, wine grapes, and even the emerald-fleshed Chinese gooseberry some promoter rechristened "kiwifruit." And then of course there's the nation's most renowned export: New Zealand lamb.

Sheep are everywhere in New Zealand, standing out on green pastures like so many cue balls on an enormous and lumpy snooker table. This nation leads the world in lamb and mutton production, and only Australia exports more wool. Between spring lambing and fall slaughter, some 100 million sheep—nearly 30 *times* the human population of the country—romp about New Zealand. The North Island's Wharekauhau Station, east of Wellington, supports some 10,000 head, mostly on rolling plateaus that drop abruptly to the sea. In springtime you can see the farm's owner, Bill Shaw, racing around muddy paddocks and making open-field tackles on week-old lambs—all so that he can dock their long tails, install ear tags, squirt them with disinfectant, and record their sex. Routine chores, perhaps, but there's something about chasing tiny lambs and coming home in muck-splashed jeans that makes you feel like a kid again—or even a rodeo cowboy. Indeed, Bill refers to the four-wheeled motorcycles he uses to muster sheep as "New Zealand quarter horses."

Raising sheep is part business, part fun. Shearing them, says Bill's full-time hired hand Joe Houghton, "is one of the most physically demanding jobs you could ever take on."

"But," Joe explained, "a New Zealander—Godfrey Bowen—turned shearing into an art form." Bowen devised and taught vastly more efficient techniques for handling and shearing the animals, such as the "sheep walk." Joe demonstrated it by grabbing a ewe, forcing her up on her hind legs and keeping her slightly off balance, so that she walked wherever

Joe desired. This little trick, he said, helps conserve a shearer's energy. To-day, the best shearers go through more than 400 head a day with electric clipping tools, the fleece deftly rolling off each sheep in a continuous mat, first one side, then the other. It's a lot like watching bananas being peeled. Competitions have evolved; this once mundane task has become a spectator sport pitting champions head-to-head. Some farms now charge admission, bolstering flagging farm profits with tourist dollars. Many more offer lodging and meals, attracting travelers with cheaper rates and more relaxed atmospheres than faceless motels might provide.

Worried that your sleeping quarters might be in the tractor shed or—worse yet—Aunt Em's room? Not at Wharekauhau, where Bill Shaw's wife, Annette, considers the farm-holiday boom "a revolution" she's determined to lead. Their newly renovated farmhouse includes several posh suites complete with costly paneling of *rimu*—a native wood—and gold-plated bath fixtures. The antique-strewn living area hardly seems the proper place for Bill's muddy gum boots. And next year, Annette plans a new, separate building that will hold five additional suites, equally lavish, increasing guest capacity to 20 people. Oh, and don't expect peanut butter or stewed mutton; evening meals, she promises, are "gourmet, four-course minimum," complemented with some of New Zealand's best wines. Her brochure never mentions the word "farm." Instead it refers to Wharekauhau as "an exclusive hideaway" where guests can fish for trout, ride a jet boat, hunt deer, snorkel for local rock lobster, take to the hills on foot or horseback, golf, canoe, windsurf, tour the seacoast by motorcycle, or—well—about the only pastime you can't partake of here is snow skiing.

One of New Zealand's lesser known—or at least less talked about—outdoor activities concerns a creature that, pound for pound, costs far more than lamb or even lobster. It's called whitebait, and its mecca is the South Island's remote west coast.

Whitebait are fish, actually five different species of the salmonid genus *Galaxia*. The Southern Hemisphere's answer to the North's trout and salmon, *Galaxia* seasonally leave the sea to swim upriver and spawn. Don't expect monster 20-pounders, however. *Galaxia* in their prime are only an inch or two long and a quarter-inch wide, traveling in large schools called shoals. Fishermen snare them with fine-mesh traps set out from the riverbank, then cook them whole and eat them en masse.

Whitebait are slightly green and totally transparent, with tiny black eyes the diameter of a common pin—the shaft, not the head. Their fins are so small they seem more eel than fish. New Zealanders usually eat them in omelet-like "patties" bound with egg. But the first time I cooked whitebait, I simply sauteed them lightly in butter all by themselves. I remember watching them turn white as spaghetti and thinking that they could in fact pass for some new pasta sensation; their minuscule black eyes and faintly dotted lateral lines looked like flecks of pepper embedded in the dough. Delicious, but the taste? Similar to delicately flavored *fettuccine al dente*, perhaps, or a subtle white cheese—definitely more texture than taste.

Farmer Bruce Buchanan of Marlborough has been whitebaiting every spring since 1947, when he and a friend first fished the upper reaches of Cascade River, on the South Island's narrow, rainy west coast.

"There was nothing here but sea gulls," he recalls. "We came in on horses, and packed the 'bait out over an old cattle track." Each trip took nine hours, one way. A few seasons later, they returned via the sea, taking a 30-foot boat in through pounding surf and up the rock-filled river.

"It was risky to carry on like that, so we made an airstrip as quickly as we could." Single-engine planes gave them easier access—not only to the river but also to the fresh market, where retail prices for whitebait make it New Zealand's most expensive delicacy.

The thrill for whitebaiters, however, lies less in profits than in the pursuit of happiness in the bush, living life as if it were some great open-air adventure. The same exhilaration drives another breed of outdoorsmen—the river runners. Professional rafter Geoff Hunt of Queenstown considers the Landsborough River on the South Island's west coast the best for rafting in all New Zealand. He likes its scenic vistas, its challenging white water, and its length. Boasting some 40 raftable miles above its confluence with the Haast River, the Landsborough makes a good three- or four-day float in a nation so vertical that most white-water trips last only hours, not days.

Taking a raft through the Landsborough with Geoff and his friends, I found, is at times like riding a mattress through a washing machine—bouncy, wet, a bit unwieldy. At one spot we clung on as the river dropped ten feet in a single waterfall, then swirled through treacherous rock gardens that left little time to take in the magnificent scenery. Stretches of slack water allowed us to regroup—and to gaze lazily at the mountain backdrop and widening banks of greenery. This is the Landsborough's alter ego, its quiet side, often accompanied by expansive beech forest.

Enter it and you enter a realm of semidarkness, shielded from the sun by a 60-foot-high canopy. It is wet and lush; every tree—standing or fallen—every rock, every branch and twig and square inch of ground draped in a gauzy cobweb of living mosses and lichens. Scientists call it rain forest, but here rain doesn't fall as much as it oozes: The near-solid canopy breaks the fall of raindrops and passes them from leaf to leaf and finally to the forest floor. Footprints of deer punctuate the mossy carpet; purple-capped mushrooms stud a green-sheathed twig; time slows.

The hoary forest serves delightful counterpoint to the Landsborough's breathtaking plunges and rugged mountain views. The river's enduring attraction—like that of New Zealand itself—lies in its variety. So sit back and let the outdoors create its scenic memories. I still recall my Landsborough trip and Geoff's words about his homeland: "It's a place where I can go raft or do anything I want, nice and close. Everything's so close to the sea—and to the mountains. The other thing about the country is a lack of people. A bit over three million is all we have, and most are in the top half of the North Island. That's fine—they can come down and visit, but basically we've got the South Island all to ourselves. Now, I *like* that. You know, we're really fortunate people."

Indeed you are, Geoff, indeed you are.

"We're pretty fortunate to be living and working in the best place in the world. We can wake up to blue sky, fresh air, clear running water, and skylarks fluttering overhead," says Charles Hasselman, a 57-year-old South Island sheep farmer. A native of the Netherlands, Hasselman came to New Zealand in 1951 seeking "a more productive life-style—one that didn't exist in postwar Holland. I took to riding horses and mustering sheep like a duck takes to water. It's like a paid holiday here." More than a century before Hasselman arrived, the island's economy began to center on sheep introduced from Australia. Native tussock grasslands and a temperate climate ideal for year-round grazing encouraged settlers—mostly British—to take up sheep farming. Profit-minded colonists exported wool until refrigerated ships made it possible to export meat. Today fertilized pastures of exotic grasses sustain as many as 100 million sheep. New Zealand leads the world in lamb and mutton production and ranks second only to neighboring Australia as the leading exporter of wool.

FOLLOWING PAGES: In the footsteps of his father, Mark Hasselman tends his flock of merinos grazing Temple Peak Station, the 18,000-acre Hasselman property on the South Island. Most high country farmers favor the merinos, of Spanish origin. Their surefootedness and heavy fleece enable them to withstand the rigors of mountain life.

*B*rooding Thompson Mountains rim
*Lake Wakatipu, plied at twilight by the
vintage steamer T.S.S. Earnslaw.
Steamships carried gold across this
South Island lake during the 1860s rush.
After the gold deposits played out, the
vessels transported provisions and
livestock to lakeshore farms inaccessible
by road. Last of its kind on New Zealand
waters, the* Earnslaw *caters to tourists.
Shipboard visitors hear of a peculiar lake
feature described in a Maori legend: A
giant sleeps at the bottom of glacier-fed
Lake Wakatipu, his heartbeat causing a
periodic rise and fall in the water level—
as much as three inches every ten
minutes in certain places. Scientists
attribute the unusual occurrence to a
combination of winds funneled by the
mountains and rapid fluctuations in
atmospheric pressure. Edging the South
Island's Eglinton Valley, near Lake Te
Anau, the Earl Mountains tumble to
fields ablaze with flowering lupine
(below)—a species introduced from
North America to brighten the valley.*

ictorian dining hall buzzes with the voices of lads enjoying roast lamb, hot vegetables, and tea at Christ College. The decorum of this secondary school echoes the Anglican heritage of Christchurch. The school dates from 1850, when John Robert Godley led English colonists to settle Christchurch near the rolling Canterbury Plains of the South Island. The community eventually became the South's major metropolis. Although considered "the most English city outside England," Christchurch still carries a rural charm, derived from its setting in the heart of the island's breadbasket. Each spring, some 90,000 spectators attend the city's Agricultural and Pastoral Show. One happy competitor, 8-year-old Belinda Price (above), gives her ribbon-winning heifer, Paisley Senator Queen, a big hug. Daughter of a fourth-generation farmer, Belinda began competing at age 4, not unusual in this agrarian region.

*L*ife imitates art at Arrowtown's Royal Oak Pub, a favorite hangout of retired farmers Bill Dennison and Paddy Mathias. A gold-rush boomtown in the 1860s, the South Island's Arrowtown now draws visitors to its restored buildings of the mining era. On the North Island, tree-lined Manaia Stream (opposite) winds through morning mist outside the town of Oromahoe. This region, rich in volcanic soil, nurtures sheep pastures and dairy farms.

*R*ounding a marker under stormy
skies, yachts race in Auckland's
Waitemata Harbour, the nation's busiest

commercial port. Every January, sails
speckle Waitemata as boats vie in the
world's largest one-day regatta. Local
crews at this event enter other
international races as well. A few have
made it to the America's Cup trials.

*S*ilver fern leaves (below), New Zealand's national emblem, fringe a track in the North Island's Urewera National Park. The preserve's 500,000 acres encompass the traditional home of the Tuhoe Maori—"Children of the Mist." Tuhoe guide Whare Biddle (below) escorts park visitors. Opposite: Feathery mamakus *shadow a glen in* Whakarewarewa State Forest Park near Rotorua. Isolated for ages, seagirt New Zealand has developed such remarkable flora as a forget-me-not with platter-size leaves and the pigmy tree, one of the world's smallest conifers; it can bear seeds when only three inches tall.

FOLLOWING PAGES: *A visitor peers into a crater of Mount Tarawera on the North Island. In 1886 the volcano exploded in the most awesome display of nature's power yet recorded in New Zealand.*

SEYCHELLES
Faraway Isles of Eden

By Christine Eckstrom Lee.   Photographs by Bill Curtsinger.

*Indian Ocean breezes refresh Mahé,
capital island of the Seychelles. These
remote isles promise hidden coves, coco-
de-mer palms, and lush hillsides scented
with flowering trees and rare orchids.*

Asong I heard in the Seychelles sings of an island lost in the middle of the sea, a place *"comme dans l'air"*—as if in the air, afloat like a cloud, somewhere between ocean and sky. The expression carries a hint of the otherworldly, an idea that befits the faraway Seychelles, a group of a hundred equatorial isles sprinkled across the western Indian Ocean like a lone constellation. Unlike most midocean islands, the main isles of the Seychelles are made of granite, heaped into steep, dark mountains of stone, weathered and furrowed like monstrous sculptures. The land is jungled with tropical forests that hold species found nowhere else on earth: coco-de-mer palms and jellyfish trees; wild vanilla orchids and yellow pitcher plants; black parrots, blue pigeons, and red-headed doves. An aura of fantasy surrounds the land. Resident artist Michael Adams, an Englishman, told me of his first impression of the Seychelles, "The islands seemed so magical, I had the feeling that around the next corner I might find a pink horse."

From the beginning, the earliest accounts of the Seychelles sounded fanciful. Explorers in the 1700s had found giant tortoises lumbering in the forests and lounging around the tops of the mountains, which rise to heights of nearly 3,000 feet on the main island of Mahé. Huge crocodiles, now extinct, climbed up there to eat them, and 18th-century settlers reported that when the winds were calm, they could hear the dreadful sound of crocodiles fighting with sharks at sea. Along the shores, early-day voyagers saw dugongs—sea mammals that brought to mind the sirens of myth—and some unusual creatures that may have been sea elephants, living far from their subantarctic range.

Even my travels in the Seychelles took on the quality of being comme dans l'air. In a world of plants and animals and sea life I had never before seen or imagined, I heard tales to rival the sorcery of the landscape. People told me stories of the giant squid, of gris-gris witchcraft and Aladdin's lamp, and of chests of treasure lost, found, or strangely transported through the hills, as if by spirits. Taking pleasure in the seemingly unreal or unexplained is part of the charm of islands, and tiny, far-off, palm-covered isles fill a niche in our imaginations. Islands like the Seychelles have the appeal of the land just over the farthest hill; they satisfy the human urge to find something new.

In the hilly heart of the island named Praslin, second largest of the Seychelles, stands a 46-acre nature reserve known as the Vallée de Mai. It is a primeval forest, musical with bird songs, that shelters one of the highest percentages of endemic species in the world. Thirty of the Seychelles' 80 species of native flora are found there, and some of the plants and animals live only in the Vallée de Mai, including the most extraordinary of the Seychelles species: the coco-de-mer palm. Standing as tall as 100 feet, with broad fronds as long as 20 feet, the coco-de-mer bears a nut that can weigh as much as 40 pounds—the largest and heaviest seed in the world.

It is said that centuries ago coco-de-mer nuts sometimes drifted ashore on the Maldive Islands, 1,300 miles northeast of the Seychelles, and that the people there believed that the double-lobed nut came from a submarine palm; so they named it coconut of the sea, *coco-de-mer* in French. Thought to be a cure-all, an antidote to poisons, and an aphrodisiac, the coco-de-mer nut was once prized from Europe to China. One legend about the source of the coco-de-mer, from an account of Magellan's voyage in 1519, said that birds large enough to carry an elephant dwelt in the palm, which arose from the sea, in a place aswirl with storms, somewhere below Java the Great. A real mystery does exist: The coco-de-mer nut rarely floats, and some historians suggest that the seafaring people of the Maldives may have known the location of the Seychelles before anyone else—and kept the Vallée de Mai a secret.

Following a narrow dirt path, I entered the Vallée de Mai in silence, as if it were a cathedral. Five black parrots whistled from a takamaka tree near the trailhead. Just a few dozen of the darkling birds remain in the world, and they are rarely seen even in the Vallée de Mai, their only home on earth. The path wound through a tunnel of outsize greenery, which included leaves of hardwoods, palms, and leggy vacoa marrons that stand as tall as 60 feet. Near the center of the valley I reached a forest of coco-de-mers. Filtered light and green shadow cast an eerie sheen on the bunches of big, heart-shaped nuts clustered in the palms.

At first there was only stillness. No one had told me about the wind, and when it began to blow, the four thousand coco-de-mers of the Vallée de Mai came alive, like the enchanted trees in *The Wizard of Oz*. Fronds swayed overhead, bashing together, and some old ones fell, cracking and tearing, down to the forest floor. As the wind increased, the forest rocked, in a dizzying scene of swinging palms and rising sound. It seemed that the ocean would come roaring in, and the effect of standing among the coco-de-mers in the wind was of an excitement verging on madness, as if I were about to be whirled up into a great vortex of gale and noise and endless green.

When the wind stopped, I sat to rest by a stream and saw in the water a coco-de-mer, its shell gone, the nut gleaming black like a talisman. The air smelled like earth and fruit, and sunbirds chittered above in the canopy, flickering among the fronds like bits of shadow. It was easy to imagine why that devout British general Charles George Gordon, who came to the valley in 1881, believed that he had found the Garden of Eden. To me, it seemed more like a world before biblical order, a land of nature ungoverned.

The first people to spot the Seychelles—or to be cast ashore there—may have been voyagers in a Portuguese caravel, a Maldivian Arab dhow, or an Indonesian sailing canoe. Lying just below the Equator 1,000 miles east of Africa, 1,700 miles southwest of India, and 650 miles north of Madagascar, the Seychelles are remote in one of the world's less traveled seas, and are off the main exploration and trade routes of the Indian Ocean. The land area of the islands totals a mere 171 square miles, less than one-half the size of Los Angeles. The Seychelles, however, are scattered across a tract of sea about the size of California, some 150,000 square miles—plenty of room for a sailing ship to chance upon an uncharted isle.

The Seychelles are so recently inhabited—the first French settlers arrived little more than two centuries ago—that the history of the isles is straightforward and unplumbed. The islands had no ancient civilizations, no indigenous peoples—no population before 1770. Historian Kantilal Jivan Shah, known to everyone as "Kanti," told me, "Tracing the genealogies of

SEYCHELLES

CURIEUSE

PRASLIN

FÉLICITÉ

VALLÉE DE MAI
NATIONAL PARK

LA DIGUE

NORTH

INDIAN
OCEAN

SILHOUETTE

0   5   10 km
0   5 mi

•Victoria

Morne
Seychellois
2,969 ft
905 m

•Cascade

MAHÉ

•Baie Lazare

*Scattered across more than 150,000
square miles of the western Indian
Ocean, the Seychelles fall into four major
clusters just below the Equator: Aldabra,
Farquhar, Amirante, and the main
archipelago—the Seychelles group
depicted on this page. Unlike the coral
cays and atolls that make up the other
three groups, the central archipelago
rises from a submarine granite plateau—
perhaps a fragment of an ancient
continental landmass.*

the Seychellois is easy. We only go back six or seven generations. The real
question is, who first saw the Seychelles? And what is hiding in the islands
that we have not yet uncovered?"

I met Kanti at Jivan Imports, his general store in the middle of Victoria, the capital of the islands. The town nestles on the isle of Mahé, where
most of the Seychelles' 65,000 people reside. Kanti lives above his shop, in a
warren of rooms filled with shelves of books and a museum collection of local artifacts: pottery, crystal, ivory; coins, bottles, porcelain; cannonballs, a
ship's brass bell—and delicate mother-of-pearl sculptures carved by Kanti.
"My house is a national monument," he said, arms outstretched, standing
amid knee-high stacks of historical volumes. "All of this is my life!"

Downstairs, Kanti is a dealer of goods; upstairs, he is a merchant of
knowledge, and he plays with what he knows. Someone said to me, "Who
knows what Kanti has buried up there in all those books and papers?" Kanti
told me, "I'm the witch doctor of the Indian Ocean. I hold the original Aladdin's lamp. I can tell you whatever you want to know."

Kanti has helped locate shipwrecks through study of his many doc-
uments, and he has a special interest in the conservation of the Seychelles'

170

natural treasures. "I even had a species named for me," he said, pointing to a clipping on a faded page in one of his scrapbooks. It described a small spider Kanti had found and sent to British naturalist Lyall Watson; this now has the scientific name *Ischnothyreus jivani*. Dr. Watson compared Kanti to "an intellectual spider that sits in the centre of a vast web of knowledge, tugging gently and curiously at the strands, just to see what happens."

Kanti's family is Indian, one of many nationalities that make up Seychelles society. Just as early voyagers came to the islands from all directions, so did the forebears of the people who live there today. Most Seychellois are descended from French settlers, people brought as slaves from Africa and Madagascar, or immigrants from India and China, and a majority of islanders have ancestors from a combination of groups.

"There is nowhere in the world that has a culture like the Indian Ocean islands," Kanti said. "Africa, Europe, and Asia met here, and were all mixed together in this great caldron of cultures. Language, food, folklore, beliefs—and people—have blended here in a beautiful new way. We are Créole, and we are unique."

The Seychelles is the only country in the world with Créole as an official national language; English and French, the other official languages, are taught in school, but Créole is most widely spoken. Seychellois Créole is based on French, but it includes Bantu, Hindi, English, and Malagasy words, making it different from Haitian, Cajun, and other créole tongues.

"The islands and the sea have made us different," Kanti said. "We live in an atmosphere of nature, and the Seychellois has developed a mentality of great freedom. In many ways, this is the last paradise," he continued. "You have only to walk in the Vallée de Mai to know. But some things here should only be brought to light if we are bound to respect them. There are things in Seychelles that shouldn't be touched for centuries to come. We should leave them for the mystery of life."

If people had lived in the islands thousands of years ago, they would have created myths about the land, especially the rocks. From the seashores to the mountaintops, gigantic rocks loom. Mounds of jumbled boulders, many the size of houses, stud the hills and frame scalloped coves around the islands. Granite monoliths rise above the palms and poke through thick forest like ancient monuments lost in green luxuriance. Some of the rocks are balanced in impossible ways, tipped up on their small ends, wedged in suspension between two walls, teetering atop each other— seemingly poised for disaster.

The outer islands of the Seychelles are geologically young coral atolls and cays, but the ancient isles of the central archipelago, which includes Mahé and Praslin, are made of granite 650 million years old. Scientists have several theories about the origin of the granite isles. One holds that they are a continental fragment left behind when India broke away from Africa and moved north, some 135 million years ago. Another speculates that the Seychelles may once have been the eastern coast of Africa.

Because no ancient people lived in the Seychelles, most of the islands and landforms are named for ships, explorers, or for 18th-century French officials. The name Seychelles honors a French comptroller general who served Louis XV, and Mahé bears the name of the man who, in the 1740s, ordered the first extensive charting of the islands. Years later, Mahé de la Bourdonnais, locked in the Bastille on charges brought by a rival governor, drew a map of the Seychelles on a handkerchief with his blood, as if to ensure that the tiny isles would be remembered.

A street name in Victoria keeps alive the memory of Jean-Baptiste Quéau de Quinssy, the ultimate pragmatic islander. The British and French were vying for control of the Indian Ocean when de Quinssy was appointed to administer the Seychelles in 1794. During the next 20 years, he was forced to capitulate to British warships seven times—and raise the Union Jack above the islands. Each time, after the British ships sailed over the horizon, he hoisted the French flag again. When the British acquired the Seychelles in 1814, de Quinssy changed his name to De Quincy, and stayed on as the new British administrator of the islands.

Since 1814, the Seychelles have changed from a dependency of the British colony of Mauritius to an independent socialist republic, and the way of life in the islands has shifted from a plantation system centered on coconut and spice production to an economy based on tourists lured by the island's greatest natural resource—beauty.

The very name of one of the tinier Seychelles suggests its chief asset. Bird Island, which lies about 60 miles north of Mahé, is home to a variety of avian species, including dainty fairy terns and finchlike Madagascar fodies. But from April to November, the 175-acre flat coral cay is the nesting ground for more than one million sooty terns. Flocks of them peppered the skies and soared in funnels above the sea when I visited Bird Island one sunny day in September. Countless young sooties, in juvenile black plumage, darkened the ground of the nesting area near the center of the island. The calls of the adults, circling and swooping, combined with the screams of the young ones in a steady din of cries that rose and fell in great waves of sound.

"It's a bit like being on a ship of birds," island owner Guy Savy told me. The island had long been famous for its birds when Guy took it over in 1967, but the land had been planted in coconut palms, for the once lucrative production of copra, and many of the birds moved away. Over the years, Guy and his wife, Marie-France, began to change the land back to the way it looked when 18th-century explorers first spied the island. The Savys removed palm trees and more sooties returned. Since 1967, the tern population has increased from fewer than 150,000 to more than one million. In the 1970s, the Savys built an airstrip, a restaurant, and bungalows for visitors who come to watch the birds.

"When I first came here, I thought that tourism was the only thing for the island—and for the birds," Guy explained, "and it has proven right. Nature and tourism can live side by side here, and I think that's an important theme for Seychelles."

Before the international airport was built, the Seychelles were a difficult destination for anyone to reach. Cruise ships called occasionally, as did the Lindblad *Explorer,* carrying passengers on voyages with natural history as their theme. Guy thinks that the impact of the *Explorer* on the Seychelles was significant.

"A lot of things happened all at once in the '60s and '70s," he said. "Conservation became an issue around the world. Tourism in the Seychelles was just beginning, and then the Lindblad *Explorer* came through with all these naturalists on board," he recalled. "And all of a sudden the tour guides here had to learn the names of the birds and the trees. Now, the emphasis on natural history in attracting tourists to Seychelles is very strong, and I think that the Lindblad *Explorer* is quite a bit responsible for introducing us to our own wildlife."

The separate worlds of nature and people and the blending of those two worlds in the Seychelles are the subjects of Michael Adams's wildly colorful paintings. His work has been exhibited in Europe, Africa, and Asia, and it is well known and appreciated in the Seychelles.

Michael lives in an old wooden planter's house on Mahé, with his wife, Heather, their two young children, and a great number of cats, ducks, and ever-crowing roosters. Surrounded by his paintings of land and life in the Seychelles, Michael told me that he first came to the islands in 1972, on the merits of an amusing story. "I was living in Kenya," he said, "and a friend in Mombasa described the islands to me. But then he said, 'Seychelles is fantastic. All the old men wear hats, and they never take them off, even when they go to bed.' I thought that was wonderful, and I found that everything was exactly as he described—even the hats."

I looked at his paintings of the island forests, the foliage lush and intricate and jeweled with colors. Many of his portraits of Seychelles life feature a mélange of motifs—symbols of India, verses from the Koran, Maya glyphs—tucked in the background, or decorating buildings and objects. "There are bits of the whole world mixed in these islands," Michael explained, "and the culture is changing all the time, with each thing that arrives—new people, imported goods, even a postcard from some faraway place. Little pieces of the world come to Seychelles," he said, "and all I'm doing is painting a diary."

Michael took me to meet Henri Dauban, one of the men in his portraits. Michael calls him "the grand old man of the islands," and "Monsieur Pourquoi—Mister Why" for his broad-ranging and questioning mind. "He sits in his chair with his eyes wide and these lovely words pour out," Michael said. "He'll tell us some tales."

Henri Dauban was born on Silhouette, one of several islands his family once owned. Through the years, he has been a planter, stockman, sailboat builder, and, like most Seychellois men, he was a fisherman. As a child he harpooned fish, "like all the little boys on the island," he said. "It was natural to me to throw a harpoon." Later, his family sent him to school in England, where he graduated from the London School of Economics. Outside London one day in 1924, he watched a group of young men throwing javelins. "To me they were harpoons," Henri said, "and they threw them so badly. So I asked if I could try." Without taking a run, he tossed the javelin twice the distance of any of the others. Within weeks, he was competing in the 1924 Olympics in Paris. Soon after, his family called him home to the Seychelles, ending what Henri called his "harpoon career"—but not his seafaring life.

Just before World War II, when Henri was living on Bird Island and managing the plantation there, he went out in a small pirogue with his men, fishing for the local barracuda called *bécune.*

"It was about half past seven and growing dark," Henri recalled, "because it is at the beginning of the night that the bécune bite. Suddenly, near to us, I saw a big mass which was about twice the length of our own pirogue. Straightaway I said, 'Well, this is a Japanese submarine.' But looking at it, I was struck by the fact that there was no conning tower, and the searchlights were red, looking like eyes—a red ring, then a white, and the centers were brown. My men wanted to cut the rope and run away.

"A few minutes later, another one came up, a bit behind the first, and bigger—about 65 feet long. There were the same two eyes, facing us again. Then a big arm came up, and then another, and I remembered that the Norwegians called these 'Kraken.' They were giant squid. Possibly it was a male and female breeding. My men took the oars, and I never saw the boat go that fast. I think, by the way my men behaved, that they must have seen the giant squid there before."

Few people have seen a giant squid. Pieces of them have washed ashore here and there and have been found in the stomachs of sperm whales, but not a single live specimen has ever been captured; the creature remains a mystery of the deep.

There is brotherhood and secrecy among fishermen, and I saw a bit of both when Henri Barrallon and André Pool invited me to go bécune fishing with them off Mahé. It was just after dark, the time when the bécune bite, and a sliver of moon had risen into the dome of southern stars. André tossed his line from the bow; Henri and I tossed ours from the stern. When I asked him what bait we were using, he only said, "Sssh."

Several pirogues of fishermen were anchored nearby. As the hours passed, some of the parties caught fish, others caught nothing—and jokes were exchanged. Suddenly one boat began to rock. The fishermen stood up, hollering and cursing: A whale shark, the biggest fish in the sea—and unusual to see anywhere in the world—was tangled in their anchor line. Although whale sharks are harmless plankton-eaters, they can weigh 15 tons. Most fishermen fear them: They have been known to overturn boats as they rub against the hulls to scrape parasites from their backs. Help was offered the fishermen, but there was no choice for them but to cut their line and go home, sacrificing their anchor.

By the end of the evening, André had hauled in six big bécune, while Henri and I had caught nothing. It was only much later that I realized that, although Henri and André were cousins and were fishing in the same boat, neither had divulged what his bait was to the other—and I still don't know what any of us used.

The Indian Ocean is the world's only great sea whose currents reverse directions with the seasons. Twice a year, while the winds and currents "turn around," the air and seas around the Seychelles become calm and perfect for diving. In late October, at the beginning of one of the turnaround times, photographer Bill Curtsinger and I set off on a diving trip to the Amirantes, small coral isles about 200 miles southwest of Mahé.

We traveled there aboard *Escapade,* a 45-foot cabin cruiser owned by Mahé resident Fred Janker. En route, Fred said of the Amirantes, "The fish are so tame they don't know how to be afraid of you. Every time I dive there, I see something I have never seen before. This is the beauty of Seychelles."

We roamed the waters of the Amirantes for several days, diving around Desroches, Poivre, St. Joseph, and D'Arros. Seen from afar, these flat islands packed with palms and casuarinas look like bone china platters heaped with greenery and placed on a turquoise cloth.

Off Desroches, where six cows strolled along a sugary beach, we descended a hundred feet to a garden of black coral, where fat jacks drifted by like blimps. On one dive a manta ray flapped past. I saw dolphins cavorting above me. In the seas off Poivre, I swam to a hawksbill turtle; it eyed me with a sidelong stare but didn't flee. Swimming beside it, I grabbed the shoulders of its shell. It took off in a burst of speed, carrying me on a racing turtle ride, the water rushing against my face like the wind.

I floated beneath schools of rainbow flashers that tumbled down a coral drop-off like waterfalls of yellow and blue, and sometimes I rested prone on the sandy bottom and watched tiny turquoise fish the length of my fingernail come over to swim in my hair. Once I dropped down to peek into a low coral cave and looked into a thousand pairs of eyes.

On a night dive off St. Joseph, we descended a wall of gorgonians and turned off our torches to see the diffuse light of the moon undersea. Several times I sat motionless underwater, next to schools of millions of tiny fry close enough to touch. If I reached out, they flinched away together, always staying just beyond my fingertips. They reflected that quality the undersea world seems to possess—a sense of being almost attainable, at the edge of understanding, but of always retaining a core of mystery.

Each dive was a blink, a snapshot of life undersea. I remember a dive off Mahé, in the very place where we had been fishing for bécune at night. I was 40 feet down, suspended in the center of a merry-go-round of bécune—curious about me—when I turned and saw a long, massive gray shape, perhaps 20 feet in length, hovering. It was a whale shark, and almost as soon as I saw it, it melted away in a sea hazy with plankton, like a messenger from a world that waits to be found.

In the Seychelles, the islands themselves still hold the elusive qualities of the undersea world. On Mahé, I once sat on a rock by a mountain road looking up at the highest peak in the islands, Morne Seychellois—a sheer wall of granite with a crown of forest. Clouds circled the mountain, but the summit rose above them, comme dans l'air. It looked like a fairy-tale castle, and I let myself think of what might be hidden up there, in a place where few people go. For a moment, the clouds opened, revealing a score of white-tailed tropic birds floating up the mountain face, riding on updrafts. I will save that memory, with the tales of Seychelles, to keep in the place in my mind where islands live.

*V*estige of British rule: A clock tower, erected on Mahé in 1903 and modeled after London's Big Ben, ticks away the hours in Victoria, capital of the Seychelles. Bunting decorates the clock for Liberation Day, the anniversary of the 1977 coup that gave the Seychelles a new and socialist government. Gentle breezes set the pace for a ferry (opposite) leaving Praslin bound for La Digue.

*P*erched for a drink, a Madagascar fody plucks a blossom and swallows nectar as it drips from the stem. Introduced to these islands around 1860, the tiny bird thrives mainly in gardens along coastal fringes. Thirteen species of birds and

80 kinds of plants, from jellyfish trees to wild vanilla orchids, live exclusively in the Seychelles.

Champion heavyweight coconut, a coco-de-mer (right) glistens in a stream in Praslin's Vallée de Mai, a national park set up to preserve the coco-de-mer palm. The tree yields a heart-shaped nut weighing as much as 40 pounds. A meadow of coco grass and beach morning glories (opposite) covers a hillside on Mahé. Weathered rocks 650 million years old distinguish the Seychelles, one of earth's rare midocean granitic island groups. At a stream near Cascade, women do their laundry, often passing the time by exchanging news. Faster than clothing can dry, information speeds through the gossip network, locally called radio bambou.

*A*fter school but still wearing their
school uniforms, two girls tarry on La
Digue. Here bicycles, oxcarts, and bare
feet track the sandy lanes of an island
still accessible only by boat. Though
Arab voyagers had probably visited the
Seychelles by the seventh century A.D.,
the isles remained uninhabited until
French settlers arrived in 1770 to start
vegetable and spice plantations. Pirates,
whalers, and traders have all come
ashore. The British governed the islands
from 1814 to 1976, when the Seychelles
became an independent republic. The
faces and life-styles of the islanders
reflect the mix of Europeans, Africans,
and Asians; this heritage gave rise to
a language and culture characterized as
Créole. In Baie Lazare on Mahé, the
Seychelles' most populous isle, a woman
(above) holds up a string of fish known
locally as maquereau—*favored for
grilled dishes.*

*B*oats beached or moored and a net being hauled ashore close out the day for fishermen on Mahé. Fishing—with traps, seines, hand and trawl lines—forms the backbone of traditional island life. In the early morning, the sound of triton-shell horns from the beaches announces the arrival of boats full of fish, and many people walk to the shore and select their dinner before trucks take the catch to market. Damsel, snappers, and other smaller fishes caught, strung,

and sold in "packets" (opposite, above)
usually make fried or grilled meals.
Islanders prepare the larger tuna,
barracuda, grouper, and red snapper for
barbecues, curries, or ragouts—
specialties of Seychellois Créole cuisine.

*I*sles of sanctuary and solitude: Sooty terns take to the air above Bird Island (below), a 175-acre coral cay 60 miles north of Mahé. During their April-to-October nesting season, more than one million migratory sooties gather on this tiny haven. The island also accommodates visitors who come to enjoy the winged spectacle. On many of the islands, wildlife conservation coexists with tourism, the mainstay of the Seychelles' economy. Two reserves in the islands have been chosen by the United Nations as World Heritage sites: Praslin's Vallée de Mai forest, home of the famous coco-de-mer palm; and remote Aldabra, an atoll with the largest population of giant tortoises in the world—160,000. Along with Aldabra, several far-flung clusters of coralline isles sprinkle the southern waters of the Seychelles. Two hundred miles southwest of Mahé, a couple (opposite) strolls through surf that sculpts a sandy islet in the Amirantes—seldom-seen isles with a last-place-on-earth beauty.

*R*ainbow flashers—known as maquereaux *to island fishermen and cooks—brighten the shallows off Mahé (right). Reef waters fringing the Seychelles teem with more than 300 species of fish, some prized for eating, others for eyeing during snorkeling and scuba excursions. The granite islands also harbor an unusual combination of undersea environments: coral reefs and marine rock formations; broad expanses of shallows and banks that fall as much as 600 feet; and the plateau drop-off, where the Indian Ocean plunges to 6,000-foot depths and where marlin, sailfish, and wahoo roam. Near shore, tiny damselfish (below) and the tasty parrot fish (far right, below) inhabit rock and coral gardens.*

FOLLOWING PAGES: *Moray eels peek out from coral a hundred feet down off the isle of Desroches in the Amirantes.*

*F*anned by palms, a cove scallops the shore of La Digue, cherished by privacy-seekers for its tranquil beaches. A snorkeler (opposite) flippers off to explore coral reefs near Île Cocos.

FOLLOWING PAGES: Beyond sunlit horizons, across a thousand empty miles of Indian Ocean, the Seychelles await dreamers and adventurers in search of soothing island worlds.

193

Water droplets cling to the delicate petals of a lotus blossom. The fragrant flower decorates garden pools on the island of Bali and is used in religious offerings; in Balinese Hindu belief it signifies the throne of God.

Notes on Contributors

Largely self-taught as a photographer, now a free lance, SAM ABELL has been covering Society assignments since 1967. Among his Special Publication credits are *Secret Corners of the World*, *The Pacific Crest Trail*, and *Still Waters, White Waters*.

LESLIE ALLEN, with the Society since 1978, is the author of *Liberty: The Statue and the American Dream*, the official book for the centennial of the Statue of Liberty, prepared by the Society as a public service.

A free lance, PAUL VON BAICH studied photography in Vienna, Austria, and has published five books, including *Light in the Wilderness*. He lives near Campbellford, Ontario.

PAUL CHESLEY resides in Aspen, Colorado, the home of Photographers/Aspen, which he helped establish. He has covered the Continental Divide, the West Coast forests, and natural wonders of Europe for Special Publications.

BILL CURTSINGER, a specialist in underwater photography, has been doing contract work for the Society since 1973. His assignments have ranged from the Pine Barrens of New Jersey to undersea life beneath Antarctic ice.

A founding member of Photographers/Aspen in Colorado, NICHOLAS DEVORE III is the Directeur De Galerie Foto Arte and is on the board of trustees of Aspen Art Museum. He has contributed to Society publications for 15 years.

RON FISHER is marking his 25th year with the Society. He has worked as a production manager, a writer, and an editor. He is the author of the Special Publica-

tions *Still Waters, White Waters*, *Our Threatened Inheritance*, and *The Appalachian Trail*. He is writing a new account of the trail, which was completed 50 years ago. *Mountain Adventure: Exploring the Appalachian Trail* is scheduled for publication in 1988.

Coauthor of *America's Atlantic Isles*, CHRISTINE ECKSTROM LEE has contributed to numerous other Special Publications, among them *Isles of the Caribbean* and *Blue Horizons: Paradise Isles of the Pacific*.

TOM MELHAM, a staff writer, has reported on outdoor wonders in many Special Publications, including *Alaska's Magnificent Parklands*. He is the author of *John Muir's Wild America*.

Staff writer THOMAS O'NEILL, who traces his ancestry to Ireland, is the author of the Special Publications *Back Roads America* and *Lakes, Peaks, and Prairies: Discovering the United States-Canadian Border*.

CYNTHIA RUSS RAMSAY, a staff writer, has contributed to dozens of Special Publications, including *Splendors of the Past*, *Our Awesome Earth*, and *Alaska's Magnificent Parklands*.

Free-lance photographer SCOTT RUTHERFORD has covered assignments for NATIONAL GEOGRAPHIC, TRAVELER, and WORLD magazines and for the Special Publication *America's Great Hideaways*. He lives in Kailua on the island of Hawaii.

MICHAEL S. YAMASHITA, a free-lance photographer based in New Jersey, has undertaken major magazine and book assignments for the Society, including the Special Publications *Splendors of the Past* and *Lakes, Peaks, and Prairies*.

Acknowledgments

Throughout the course of this project the staff enjoyed the cooperation of the men and women of the National Oceanographic and Atmospheric Administration, the Nature Conservancy, and the Smithsonian Institution. The Special Publications Division is grateful to them and to the individuals and organizations named or quoted in the book. It also thanks consultants who gave generously of their time and expertise for each chapter: *Introduction:* William V. Sliter. *Galápagos:* Juan Black, Judy Carvalhal, Jerry Emory, Margarita Angermeyer de Larrea, Dieter and Mary Plage, Marsha Sitnik. *Japan:* Michael Cooper, Anne Imamura, Masayuki Itonaga, Masako Kubota, Peter Nosco, David Plath, Chako Sugi-Bellamy. *Ireland:* Paddy Derivan, Steven Ellis, Oliver L. Foley, Ian J. Hill, James Lydon, Ciarán MacMathúna, Tony Moylan, Paschal G. Mullery, Seamus O'Cathain, Marilyn Throne. *Bali:* Carl Burman, A.A.M. Djelantik, Ella Helmi, I Gusti Ayu Puspawati. *New Zealand:* Judith Binney, Kenneth J. Larsen, Hirini (Sidney) Moko Mead, Patricia H. Parata, Norrey Ann Simons. *Seychelles:* Willy André, Keith and Marivonne Berke, Lindsay Chong-Seng, Anna S. L. Fayon, Brian Kensley, Thérèse LaBlache, Philip Marzocchi, Jean C. Walden.

Additional Reading

The reader may consult the *National Geographic Index* for related articles. Also, *Islands* magazine offers pertinent material, as do the following books:

William H. Amos, *Wildlife of the Islands;* William Beebe, *Galápagos: World's End;* Jane Belo (ed.), *Traditional Balinese Culture;* Frederica M. Bunge (ed.), *Japan—A Country Study;* Sherwin Carlquist, *Island Biology;* E. Estyn Evans, *The Personality of Ireland;* Insight Guides, *Bali;* M. H. Jackson, *Galápagos: A Natural History Guide;* Paul Johnson, *Ireland: A Concise History;* Brendan Lehane, *The Companion Guide to Ireland;* Guy Lionnet, *The Seychelles;* Margaret Orbell, *The Natural World of the Maori;* Diana and Jeremy Pope, *The Mobil Illustrated Guide to New Zealand;* Edwin O. Reischauer, *The Japanese.*

INDEX

Library of Congress CIP Data
Majestic island worlds.
   Bibliography: p.
   Includes index.
   1. Islands. 2. Voyages and travels.
I. National Geographic Society (U.S.) Special Publications Division.
G500.M34 1987 910'.0914'2 87-15420
ISBN 0-87044-625-8 (regular edition)
ISBN 0-87044-630-4 (library edition)

Composition for *Majestic Island Worlds* by the Typographic section of National Geographic Production Services, Pre-Press Division. Printed and bound by Holladay-Tyler Printing Corp., Rockville, Md. Film preparation by Catharine Cooke Studio, Inc., New York, N.Y. Color separations by Lanman Progressive Company, Washington, D.C.; Lincoln Graphics, Inc., Cherry Hill, N.J.; and NEC, Inc. Nashville, Tenn.